THE LITTLE BOOK OF

Youth Engagement in Restorative Justice

Published titles include:

The Little Book of Restorative Justice: Revised & Updated,
by Howard Zehr

The Little Book of Conflict Transformation, by John Paul Lederach

The Little Book of Family Group Conferences, New-Zealand Style, by
Allan MacRae and Howard Zehr

The Little Book of Strategic Peacebuilding, by Lisa Schirch

The Little Book of Strategic Negotiation,
by Jayne Seminare Docherty

The Little Book of Circle Processes, by Kay Pranis

The Little Book of Contemplative Photography, by Howard Zehr

The Little Book of Restorative Discipline for Schools, by Lorraine
Stutzman Amstutz and Judy H. Mullet

The Little Book of Trauma Healing, by Carolyn Yoder

The Little Book of Biblical Justice, by Chris Marshall

The Little Book of Restorative Justice for People in Prison,
by Barb Toews

The Little Book of Cool Tools for Hot Topics,
by Ron Kraybill and Evelyn Wright

El Pequeño Libro de Justicia Restaurativa, by Howard Zehr

The Little Book of Dialogue for Difficult Subjects,
by Lisa Schirch and David Campt

The Little Book of Victim Offender Conferencing,
by Lorraine Stutzman Amstutz

The Little Book of Restorative Justice for Colleges and Universities, by
David R. Karp

The Little Book of Restorative Justice for Sexual Abuse, by Judah
Oudshoorn with Michelle Jackett and Lorraine Stutzman Amstutz

*The Big Book of Restorative Justice: Four Classic Justice &
Peacebuilding Books in One Volume,* by Howard Zehr, Lorraine
Stutzman Amstutz, Allan MacRae, and Kay Pranis

The Little Book of Transformative Community Conferencing,
by David Anderson Hooker

The Little Book of Restorative Justice in Education,
by Katherine Evans and Dorothy Vaandering

The Little Book of Restorative Justice for Older Adults,
by Julie Friesen and Wendy Meek

The Little Book of Race and Restorative Justice, by Fania E. Davis

The Little Book of Racial Healing,
by Thomas Norman DeWolf, Jodie Geddes

The Little Book of Restorative Teaching Tools,
by Lindsey Pointer, Kathleen McGoey, and Haley Farrar

The Little Book of Police Youth Dialogue
by Dr. Micah E. Johnson and Jeffrey Weisberg

The Little Books of Justice & Peacebuilding present, in highly
accessible form, key concepts and practices from the fields of
restorative justice, conflict transformation, and peacebuilding. Written
by leaders in these fields, they are designed for practitioners, students,
and anyone interested in justice, peace, and conflict resolution.

The Little Books of Justice & Peacebuilding series is a cooperative
effort between the Center for Justice and Peacebuilding of Eastern
Mennonite University and publisher Good Books.

THE LITTLE BOOK OF

Youth Engagement in Restorative Justice

Intergenerational Partnerships for Just and Equitable Schools

EVELÍN AQUINO, HEATHER BLIGH MANCHESTER, AND ANITA WADHWA

Good Books

New York, New York

Good Books books may be purchased in bulk at special discounts for
sales promotion, corporate gifts, fund-raising, or educational purposes.
Special editions can also be created to specifications. For details, contact
the Special Sales Department, Good Books, 207 West 36th Street, 11th
Floor, New York, NY 10018 or info@skyhorsepublishing.com.
Good Books is an imprint of Skyhorse Publishing, Inc.®, a Delaware
corporation.

Visit our website at www.goodbooks.com

10 9 8 7 6 5 4 3 2 1

Library of Congress Cataloging-in-Publication Data is available on file.

Series editor: Barbara Toews
Cover photograph: Howard Zehr

Print ISBN: 978-1-68099-748-4
eBook ISBN: 978-1-68099-770-5

Printed in the United States of America

Contents

Introduction

There's no such thing as neutral education. Education either functions as an instrument to bring about conformity or freedom.[1]

—*Paolo Freire*

This book is a call to action for restorative justice practitioners committed to building just and equitable schools in partnership with youth, families, and community. Just as there is no neutral education, there is no neutral restorative justice; solely focusing on healing interpersonal conflicts in schools through restorative justice does not acknowledge the legacy of harm in our educational system. Rooted in the wisdom of ancestral and Indigenous cultures, restorative justice (RJ) is a way of being and a philosophy grounded in community building, healing, and justice that has grown into a movement to transform schools and society.

The goal of restorative justice in education is "creating just and equitable learning environments, nurturing healthy relationships, and repairing harm and transforming conflict."[2] In this book, we push the field to go beyond "transforming conflict" to transforming the entire education system. Intergenerational partnerships, where all members of school communities collaborate with each other to create just and equitable learning environments, are at the root of this work.

Young people across the country are organizing for equitable education and RJ in schools, garnering wins through the elimination of punitive school discipline, the implementation of restorative justice, and the incorporation of Ethnic Studies into the curriculum. The purpose of this book is to illuminate a theory and practice of youth engagement in restorative justice through intergenerational partnerships where young people are agents of change.

Inequity in Schools

Restorative justice in schools addresses interpersonal harm but often fails to address larger systemic harms that result from institutional and structural injustice. Institutional injustice in schools occurs at a high level and includes policies and practices that harm people of color, students with disabilities, and those who identify as part of the LGBTQ+ community. For example, high-stakes testing companies continue to make billions of dollars to simply reinforce, and not remove, academic opportunity gaps for students of color. School closures funnel students from one low-performing school to another, and do not address root causes of socioeconomic inequity. Meanwhile, legislators nationwide have pushed to ban Ethnic Studies, an interdisciplinary field that honors the cultural and historical narratives of people who have been pushed to the margins and critically analyzes inequities to promote social change. Structural racism includes larger societal forces that reinforce inequality for people of color, including redlining, the disparate criminalization of people caught with marijuana vs. cannabis entrepreneurs, and a health care system based on profit.

Restorative justice (RJ) in schools often mirrors these inequities; when RJ is introduced for disciplinary purposes only ("restorative discipline"), it acts as a tool to maintain the status quo of adult control and compliance; adults replicate hierarchical power dynamics by lecturing at students in healing Circles. Youth are seen as merely participants in a Circle, or at most, RJ youth leaders who keep Circle in response to disciplinary incidents—not as community builders, trainers, and policy and decision makers.

The Call for Youth Engagement

This book provides a framework to explore ways that educators can learn how to work *with* young people to create just and equitable schools, rather than simply using restorative justice as a form of discipline to do *to* students. Adult RJ practitioners are sometimes lauded for their peacemaking skills and ability to connect with youth. Yet, once they leave, the work falls apart. While we believe in the necessity of dedicated adult leadership, we also believe that restorative justice is most impactful when power is shared and youth have genuine ownership. Youth are critical to the success of shifting school culture, and working in partnership with young people is an opportunity for collective growth and leadership development.

We, the three authors, have extensive experience working with youth and engage in restorative justice as a means to build social, emotional, academic, and leadership skills for personal and systematic healing.

Wadhwa, a teacher of 14 years, engages with the work as a way to heal herself and address the oppression she witnessed in the public school system as the daughter of Punjabi immigrants. Manchester, born fist first, a lifelong learner, and experiential educator, grew up impacted by stories of injustice and joy that were not part of the standard curriculum, and now partners with young people to reclaim spaces that have traditionally excluded them. Aquino, a lifetime educator and cultural worker, honors her duty to consistently work with young people to make sustainable changes in ourselves, schools, communities, and society, on the road toward collective liberation.

To us, restorative justice is not merely a program, but a movement rooted in the work of our ancestors and Indigenous teachers that will impact future generations. We honor that our specific understanding of Circles in schools—including traditions of the centerpiece and talking piece—has been shared with us by Tlingit, Tagish, First Nations, and Yukon elders. We intentionally name the communities who taught us as opposed to the blanket statement that RJ comes from "Indigenous people." We also recognize that students bring their own ancestral wisdom and may offer other ways of being in Circle. Restorative justice is meant to be transformative, and each Circle is an opportunity to shift an entire school system by strengthening community, promoting equity of voice, and offering a viable alternative to exclusionary disciplinary practices.

Based on our years of work partnering with young people and adults to build more equitable schools, we saw the opportunity to look at our specific geographic contexts, draw connections between our pedagogy, and build a collective theory and practice around youth engagement in restorative justice. We explored what it means to truly collectively write a book, while leaning into our Circle values and metaphorically passing the talking piece across our regions. We interviewed and continuously consulted young people who not only gave feedback but also contributed to the writing. They are quoted throughout the book. Our hope is that this will add a necessary dialogue to the restorative justice landscape, lifting the voices of youth and adults on the front line. We invite you to reflect on your approach in shifting paradigms and how you are engaging and sharing power with young people.

Overview of Book

We begin the book by discussing the field of Youth Engagement and ground our framework in Adam Fletcher's "Ladder of Student Involvement," a model that distinguishes between various levels of engagement with young people, beginning with tokenism and ending in youth-adult equity. We refer to this diagram throughout the book as a way to delineate the varied ways to work alongside young people to reconstruct educational institutions.

In chapter 2, we highlight the core values of youth engagement in restorative justice: intergenerational partnerships and liberatory education. We define intergenerational partnerships as engagement across generations, not solely between adults and youth but also between high schoolers and middle school students, as well as between alumni and current students. Liberatory education is education rooted in *liberation*, or freedom from practices that obstruct opportunities based on race, religion, sexual orientation, or any other identity. To achieve just schools, it is imperative that educators and youth teach with the goal of honoring every person in their humanity.

In chapter 3, we introduce Barbara Love's "Framework to Develop a Liberatory Consciousness," a tool that consists of four steps to help practitioners deepen their commitment to justice: awareness, analysis, accountability, and action. Engaging in this reflective cycle allows practitioners to examine their current practices, awareness of social conditions, identities, and ways of thinking so they can transform themselves and schools.

In chapter 4, we outline the internal work critical for combating adultism—the practice and philosophy of adults exerting power over youth, with little regard for their voice or agency. Examples of adultism at the interpersonal and institutional level are provided so that adults understand how power imbalance manifests in all levels of society. We offer reflective questions and strategies for creating models of restorative justice and Circles that involve the participation and leadership of young people and community members.

In chapters 5–8, we provide a typology of youth engagement in restorative justice that includes the various roles youth embody in restorative justice as organizers, curriculum writers, teachers, and trainers. We explore these roles in case studies from our respective cities. In Houston, high school students teach a restorative justice leadership course. In Western Massachusetts, students shift school culture through participatory action research and with support of an intergenerational community advisory board. In Oakland, young people are not only restorative practitioners and Circle keepers, but staff, policy makers, organizers, and coauthors in this book.

Chapter 9 amplifies the voices of young people from all three coasts as the young people reflect on their learnings in restorative justice, revealing key elements of restorative leadership that involve deep listening, Circle keeping, agency, self and community care, accountability, and authentic community building.

In chapter 10 we propose an emerging framework, a "Spiral of Youth Engagement," a lens that incorporates the need to understand structural injustice when moving toward youth adult-equity in full partnership. We combine elements of Fletcher's Ladder and Love's Framework, and offer liberation as the end goal of youth and adults working toward just and equitable schools.

In chapter 11, we end with a call to action for adult and youth restorative justice practitioners to work collectively to dismantle injustices and dream of the possibilities of RJ in schools. Interspersed throughout the book are reflective activities that people across generations can jointly complete in order to create a vision of just and equitable schools.

Terminology and Stylistic Choices
Because language is an indicator of one's philosophy and commitment to restorative justice, we explain a few of our stylistic choices below.

- We use "restorative justice" instead of "restorative practices," which is neutered from what we see is the end goal of the work: justice and equity.

- As race is socially constructed, so too is the verbiage around racial categories, which continues to evolve. While we understand there are critiques of the following terms, we include this explanation to be transparent about our choices:

   When indicating a person's race, we choose the lowercase "white" (to indicate those who are or perceived to be of European descent) and the uppercase "Black" (for people who are or perceived to be of African descent) in order to upend power dynamics associated with these categories. We use the term "people of color" for those who do not identify as white as most of the young people we work with do not associate themselves with the more recent term BIPOC (Black, Indigenous, People of Color). Our students varied in their use of "Latinx" and Latino/a so we use the terminology they chose to define themselves (i.e., "Guatemalan," "Dominican," "Puerto Rican").

- We capitalize Indigenous, when used to describe people, as a statement to honor the original inhabitants of the land on which we stand. We lowercase indigenous in order to describe traditions that have impacted who we are, and which we continue to learn from.

- We capitalize "Circles" in order to honor the Indigenous roots of the process and the sacred aspect of being in community with one another.
- As a small way of honoring people's dignities and respecting their humanity, we include the pronouns of the people who contributed to this book.

Chapter 1
The Field of Youth Engagement

Young people have always been at the vanguard
for community and social change, and today's
young people are no different.
—Shawn Ginwright and Taj James[1]

Youth engagement in restorative justice in schools
creates spaces for personal and societal transformation and honors that young people are resilient
social actors, participating in their communities as
leaders and peacebuilders. Adults do not "give youth
voice"; students have agency and demonstrate it in
ways others might not understand. Young people
engage all the time, whether it is convenient for
adults or not.

Youth engagement in RJ transcends involving
youth only as Circle keepers. This work takes time,
deep reflection, continuous relationship building, and
intentional strategizing with youth as partners. In this
chapter, we provide a brief overview of the field of
youth participation and integrate this knowledge into

1

our definition of youth engagement in restorative justice. We close by introducing Adam Fletcher's Ladder of Student Involvement as a tool for practitioners to push beyond tokenism as they meaningfully work alongside youth in restorative justice.

The Field of Youth Engagement

Youth participation is an international interdisciplinary field that includes subfields such as youth work, youth development, youth voice, youth organizing, youth adult partnerships, and youth engagement:

> Through active participation, young people are empowered to play a vital role in their own development, as well as in that of their communities, helping them to learn vital life-skills, develop knowledge on human rights and citizenship, and to promote positive civic action.[2]

Youth participation, a right under Article 12 of the United Nations Convention on the Rights of the Child (UNCRC), involves young people in the institutions and decisions that affect their lives. Youth participation[3] includes young people organizing for "social and political action" around issues such as education reform, juvenile justice, and climate change. The subfields of youth-adult partnerships, youth organizing, and youth engagement are particularly salient to intergenerational work with youth in restorative justice.

Effective youth participation is grounded in meaningful *youth-adult partnerships* in which youth and adult perspectives are collectively valued in any decision-making process, and the goal of strengthening community and addressing social justice issues.[4]

2

Youth organizing in education has emerged as a participation strategy for young people to build collective power and transform institutions and policies around school-based issues such as safety, policing, school closure, finance, restorative justice, and discipline policies.[5]

Youth-adult partnerships and youth organizing are both part of *youth engagement,* which most clearly captures the mechanisms by which we engage with youth in school-based restorative justice. Youth engagement is the "meaningful participation and sustainable involvement of young people in shared decisions in matters which affect their lives and those of their community, including planning, decision-making, and program delivery."[6] This is grounded in intentional partnerships, where all contributions are valued and power is shared. Students are long-term partners and decision makers in the implementation of restorative justice in schools and other spaces that affect their communities.

Currently youth engagement in RJ can be tokenistic, where an adult asks a student to co-keep a Circle they did not craft, for example. By contrast, we define youth engagement in restorative justice as *the meaningful participation of youth who are most impacted by structural injustice as changemakers and practitioners in all aspects of restorative justice—including community building, healing, and the transformation of self and institutions.* In our definition, the term *participation* is prefaced by the word *meaningful*—students do not flourish as token partners in this work, but as initiators of changes in policy and school structures. We define *youth* as any students who are of K–12 school age. By "of age," we acknowledge that many

3

youth who are pushed out of schools are still engaged in restorative justice work. By *structural injustice*, we refer to ideologies, institutions, policies, and practices that limit opportunities for people identified as disabled, undocumented, LGBTQ+, Black, Indigenous, or of color—all populations who are disproportionately punished and/or pushed out of schools.

The Ladder of Student Involvement in Schools

Adam Fletcher's Ladder of Student Involvement in Schools[7] (hereafter referred to as "The Ladder") offers a lens to imagine possibilities for transformative youth engagement in RJ. The eight-rung Ladder is divided into three levels of Youth Engagement: engaging, involving, and disengaging. The engaging levels are where work is done in partnership *with* youth, the involving levels where work is done *for* youth, and the disengaging level is where things are done *to* youth.

Fletcher does not suggest the Ladder represents work done in an entire school system; it a tool to examine and strengthen specific activities of youth engagement in schools, as well as build and use our reflective muscles. Below, we give examples of how youth engagement in restorative justice is enacted at each rung of the ladder, starting at the bottom and working our way up. (Note all examples depend on the intention of the adult in each scenario, and some actions can span different rungs of the ladder).

Manipulation: The lowest level of youth engagement, manipulation occurs when youth are coerced to participate, often through extrinsic motivation such as adult acceptance, extra credit, or money.

LADDER OF STUDENT INVOLVEMENT IN SCHOOLS

8. Student/Adult Equity

7. Completely Student-Driven

6. Student/Adult Equality

5. Students Consulted

4. Students Informed

3. Tokenism

2. Decoration

1. Manipulation

Adapted by Adam Fletcher (2011) from work by Roger Hart, et al. (1994)

Example: When students are mandated to be in a circle for class credit, or are given extra credit points if they speak during Circle as a means to create engagement. The outcome is often for the benefit of the adult, not the student.

Decoration: Occupying the second-to-last rung is the idea of young people as decorations—they are present without any meaningful involvement. This occurs when youth appear on the cover of the brochure but not at the decision-making table, or when youth are asked to attend adult-designed activities without any training or preparation. These actions are performative.

Example: When adults invite youth to photo opportunities or meetings in an attempt to appear as though they are engaging youth regularly and support youth voice.

Tokenism: At this rung, young people are at the table; however, they are often part of an adult-dominated place where they are expected to code switch and act like adults. It is a type of youth participation for show, where young people have little to no influence over the activities. In addition, it is where one young person is expected to represent all students based solely on their personal experience, as opposed to being empowered to represent the collective voice of students.

Example: In Circle keeping, tokenism can be when a student is pulled in at the last minute to "co-keep" a Circle. They are handed the agenda and assigned a role, and did not participate in planning. They lead the check-in question and a game. The adult thanks the youth. There is no debriefing the Circle.

Youth Informed: This is when student input is solicited with the facade of youth voice. Adults decide how little or how much they will be influenced by students' input and maintain full authority on the outcomes of an endeavor. Students do not know in advance that this is the decision-making structure.

Example: Youth are invited to participate in a meeting with the superintendent without being prepped. The administrators then say they held a RJ youth listening campaign; however, they never let the youth know whether their feedback was incorporated or credited.

Youth Consulted: At this step, adults actively ask youth for their ideas and thoughts in a meaningful way; however, adults still make the final decisions. Youth can be given responsibility for individual parts of an activity. Youth can substantially transform adults' opinions and actions; however, they are only given the authority that adults allow. Students know that this is the decision-making structure in advance.

Example: Youth are asked to speak at a school board meeting on restorative justice budget priorities. Their presentation may influence the board; however, final decisions are made without their vote.

Note: Youth consulted and youth informed are the most common levels of youth engagement in schools; a young person's opinions are asked for, an engagement box is checked, and adults in power make the final decisions.

Youth/Adult Equality: Youth and adults have a 50/50 split of decision-making authority, workload, and follow through. All activities are coled and equally represented by youth and adults, who make collective decisions. While this might seem ideal, it expects identical contributions without taking into account the skills and unique talents of both youth and adults.

Example: The RJ facilitator and RJ peer leader are asked to hold a Circle in an English class that is struggling to build community. They talk to the class teacher and a few students in the class to get a better idea of the needs of the class community. Alongside the teacher they co-design, co-keep, and co-debrief the Circle.

Completely Student-Driven (Youth-Led, Youth-Driven): At this rung, actions are planned, implemented, and evaluated by youth who are fully accountable to the outcomes. Adults are not in positions of authority; rather they support students in advisory and behind-the-scenes roles.

Example: Students decide to organize a sit-in at school, followed by a series of Circles, to bring attention to police brutality. As they are planning, they approach the adult RJ coordinator for support. The RJ coordinator asks them guiding questions behind the scenes to help them consider logistics and strategies for them to meet the objective of the action.

Youth/Adult Equity: In this rung, power is shared, and both youth and adults initiate actions. Both are recognized for their work and own the outcomes. The split of power and tasks varies depending on what is needed. Young people have access to spaces and information that adults do not, and vice versa. This rung is where all are aware and respect the knowledge and experiences each brings to the work and support each other to continue to grow and learn.

Example: The RJ Team on campus, which consists of Middle School Peer RJ Leaders and the school's adult RJ coordinator, agrees on different roles in order to implement a series of Circles in advisory classes. Their process is broken down to illustrate youth/adult equity in practice:

- *RJ peer leaders participate in Circles, and are trained in restorative justice and Circle keeping. The youth design Circle agendas and get feedback from the RJ coordinator.*
- *The RJ Team co-writes letters to staff and the principal, proposing Circles in advisories.*
- *The RJ Team talks to the principal to get administrative support and buy-in and emails the staff.*
- *RJ peer leaders check in with their teachers and propose a day and time for Circle during advisory while the RJ coordinator manages the scheduling and communication.*
- *The RJ coordinator writes passes to support peer RJ leaders to be excused from their classes and pick up supplies to keep advisory Circles.*
- *The RJ Team debriefs the Circles and the implementation process.*
- *The RJ Team gets feedback from students and teachers about the Circles and process.*
- *The RJ team meets with the administrative team to report back on learning and successes.*

We recognize that at various moments in time, different rungs in the middle of the ladder are not only important but also necessary to engage youth in the adult-centric structures of the education system.

9

These lower rungs can serve as necessary entry points. To reiterate, it is the *intention* that shapes where an action falls on the Ladder. When the Ladder is applied to restorative justice in schools, it gives RJ practitioners—youth and adults who work together—a lens to strengthen youth engagement in RJ as they move toward equitable partnerships.

Limitations of the Ladder

The Ladder gives us a place to start and reflect on our work, the systems we are working in, and the power we have as adults and youth as we strive for youth engagement in RJ in schools. However, the Ladder is not a stand-alone tool; it is ableist in construct and is missing a critical lens that examines the root causes of cultural and historical injustices laden in the structure of schools. Picture working in the fields at dawn, harvesting fruit from trees. Do you stand on one rung of the ladder, or do you move up and down, sometimes picking fruit off the ground or jumping off so that you can climb the tree? This metaphor allows us to understand the myriad ways one often navigates the Ladder. However, one must also be aware of the environment and agricultural practices. Who lives on, works on, and "owns" the land? How old is the tree, what is the ecosystem it is growing in and what will the fruit be used for? Whose family does it support? What enriches the soil? Youth engagement in RJ requires examining the environment of the orchard. The Ladder does not exist in a vacuum, but in conditions that are both unnatural and constructed by adults. After introducing the core values of youth engagement in chapter 3, we explore ways to reflect on and analyze these conditions.

Using the Ladder to reflect on your RJ work

- Write down the RJ activities you do on individual Post-it Notes.
- Place each one on the rung of the Ladder that matches the level of youth engagement in that activity.
- Think about what is needed to move the activity to a different part of the Ladder.
- Set aside your reflection. Invite a youth you partner with to repeat the activity.
- Write down all the activities you do together, and collectively decide where to place them on the Ladder. Get curious and discuss why you might place them on different rungs and where and how to move them to another rung.

Chapter 2
Core Values: Intergenerational Partnerships and Liberatory Education

> Intergenerational partnerships acknowledge the wisdom in every human being, moving beyond youth and adults. They include babies, children, teenagers, young adults, elders, and every age group. Everyone has something to offer to the collective, and in our journey towards justice and equity in this world we all have a role, no matter our age.
>
> —*Itzamar Carmona Felipe, RJ Alum, Oakland*

In the Civil Rights Movement, activist Claudette Colvin was only fifteen when she refused to get up from the white section of the bus, nine months before the Montgomery Bus Boycott. Secretary of the NAACP Youth Council, she was inspired by what she was learning at school during what was then called

Negro History Month.[1] Feeling that "her head was too filled with Black History," she states that she could feel the connection to abolitionists from the past as she chose her own moment of resistance:

"It felt like Sojourner Truth was on one side pushing me down, and Harriet Tubman was on the other side of me pushing me down. I couldn't get up."

Her connection to those who came before and after and her schooling around injustice speak to the two core values that guide youth engagement in restorative justice: partnerships across generations and the role of education in fighting injustice.

We begin by noting the important distinction between "youth-adult partnerships" and our first core value, intergenerational partnerships. We then define the second core value of liberatory education, and end with tips for youth and adults to consider when building intergenerational partnerships.

Core Value 1: Intergenerational Partnerships *with* Youth

Intergenerational partnerships, where all community members in and out of school communities collaborate to create just and equitable learning environments, are at the root of youth engagement in restorative justice. Youth-adult partnerships in restorative justice go beyond the binary of only youth and adults working together. In our framing, partnerships are *intergenerational* and occur when high school RJ leaders partner with middle and elementary youth; middle school RJ leaders train elementary students; alumni mentor RJ youth leaders; and elders from the community bring training and wisdom to Circles in and out of schools. *Intergenerational partnerships* are "based on an understanding of the interdependent, symbiotic nature of learning and teaching and recognizing that both youth and adults have something different, yet equally valuable to share with each other."[2]

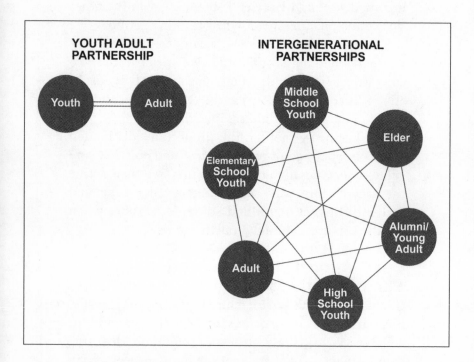

Our framing of youth engagement in restorative justice speaks to our interconnectedness and underscores the need for people across generations to work *with* each other. Dorothy Vaandering's Relationship Window[3] demonstrates the different approaches that exist in how people—youth, in our case—are regarded. She frames working *with* students as an opportunity for adults and youth to build and restore relationships through high levels of support not just for behavior, but to be honored as people. Young people are not to be "managed," "ignored," or seen as "objects of need"; they, like adults, are valued in their humanity.

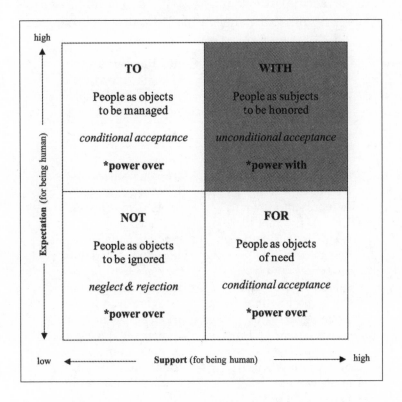

We suggest that working *with* young people requires involving them in cocreating their schools to be equitable and just. The work is reciprocal—not only youth-led or adult-led. We all have different gifts to offer, and youth are not token actors in restorative justice work, but advocates for culturally relevant curriculum, mental health supports, the implementation of community-building Circles, and the removal of police from schools. We center our work in Circle practice to disrupt hierarchical structures of leadership in schools that have traditionally marginalized youth voices. The framing of the Ladder, which distinguishes work done in partnership *with* youth, *for* youth, and *to* youth, overlaps with the four panes in the Relationship Window.

Building Intergenerational Partnerships[4]	
With the adults or youth you work with, discuss the suggestions below and add your own.	
Suggestions for adults	**Suggestions for youth**
• An individual can only represent themselves. Do not expect one youth to represent all youth. • Understand that there is a difference between doing something *with* youth and doing something *for* youth. • Treat youth with respect when engaging in conversation. Be careful to not interrupt or speak over youth when they are speaking. • Be mindful of the amount of space you are taking up. • Listen to students' opinions and concerns, and take them seriously. • Young people are busy, so be mindful of their other life responsibilities.	• Remember that adults are your colleagues. They are there to provide you support if you need help. • Practice patience while engaging with adults; they are learning too. • Share your ideas and thoughts even if they are different from the opinions of adults. • Be honest with the adults you are working with. Be vocal about your concerns regarding the decision-making process. • Be open to learning different ways to have clear communication with adults. • Be yourself because your experience and knowledge is valuable

Core Value 2: Liberatory Education in Order to Transform Structural Injustice

Liberatory education stems from the concept of *liberation*—the witnessing of others in their full humanity, outside any hierarchy, and experiencing unity while working to end oppression. Rebecca Eunmi Haslam's and Lauren Allen's diagram of *equality vs. equity vs. justice vs. liberation*[5] offers a visual by which to begin to explore liberation. One can envision these people as students, the crates as institutional supports, the fence as institutional barriers, and the band beyond the fence as the goal of liberation. In the first panel, four people of similar heights have access to crates of the same height ("equality"). However, they do not begin on an equal plane; one person is at ground level, while the other people are at sunken levels, signifying that some people have an advantage just because of where they are positioned. In the second panel those same attendees have different quantities of crates to account for their varied positions on the ground, and can now all see over the fence at the same eye level ("equity"). In the third panel, all four join forces to rip down the fence ("justice"), and in the final panel, all four revel in enjoying the band, and the ground has become level ("liberation").

So it is with youth engagement with RJ in schools— the goal is to tear down the fence and level the ground to ensure all students are honored and able to participate in just, equitable, and liberatory learning environments. The uneven ground and fence are unjust and inequitable educational policies and practices as well as the sociopolitical, economic, and cultural conditions that negatively impact young people and their communities. To be *liberated,* all people—those who have privilege, and those who do not—are freed from ideologies that place value by gender, race, religion, sexual orientation, ability, age, and a host of other factors. In other words, the fence and uneven ground of structural inequality no longer exists.

We cannot dismantle systems of oppression if we do not know they exist, so students and adults must develop an awareness of them. Educational theorist Paulo Freire defined the continuous cycle of

18

reflecting on and acting against systems of oppression as *praxis*.[6] In praxis we identify systemic injustice, reflect on where it comes from and how it is enacted, and then collectively identify what we will do to counter oppression. The ultimate goal of praxis is to liberate ourselves from our social programming so that we can see and honor all humans; whatever we teach is rooted in the goal of freedom for all people. Thus, we define *liberatory education* as *a pedagogy where adults and youth engage in praxis in order to collectively imagine and work toward a just society.*

Restorative justice has the potential to push for conditions and policies in schools that honor every member of the community. To value young people's cultures and lived experiences, RJ in education must be grounded in liberatory education—but this can only happen when young people and elders come together to help tear down the fence that inhibits us all from experiencing liberation. To truly shift school culture, both core values are essential.

The Ladder explicitly addresses the need to deepen intergenerational partnerships, but fails to address the process of reflection needed to move up and down and beyond the rungs. We devote the next chapter to our second core value of liberatory education through the introduction of Barbara Love's Framework to Develop a Liberatory Consciousness, which provides four steps of praxis that will help us reflect on how best to partner across generations.

Chapter 3
Developing a Liberatory Consciousness

> If you have come here to help me, you are wast-
> ing your time. But if you have come because
> your liberation is bound up with mine, then let
> us work together.
> —*Aboriginal rights activists in Queensland*[1]

To continue exploring the value of liberatory education, we revisit the fruit-harvesting metaphor
from chapter 2. We have to consider what socially
created conditions contribute to the orchard sur-
rounding the tree. The environment in too many of
our schools and classrooms, much like the climate of
our society, has been, and continues to be, riddled
with inequities. The soil of the orchard has been
contaminated with racism, classism, colonialism, and
other oppressions making it almost non-conducive to
nourishing trees. Historically, schools were designed
to teach compliance and skills to a population that
would be subjugated to create a working class. Now,
teachers follow scripted curriculums disconnected

from the lives of the students. Standardized testing defines ultimate success. The COVID-19 pandemic exacerbated and exposed the harsh realities of our education system; lack of access to technology and social supports alienated many students who were already on the margins.

While Fletcher's Ladder is a useful tool for reflecting on power and privilege when working with youth in RJ, the visual of a "ladder" lacks the *context* in which one moves up and down the rungs to work in intergenerational partnerships.

To give life to the value of creating just and equitable schools requires the development of a mindset geared toward liberation. Barbara Love's Framework to Develop a Liberatory Consciousness offers a lens from which to examine this context—the orchard, the soil, and the conditions in which a tree flourishes. Love defines liberatory consciousness as an awareness "that enables humans to maintain an awareness of the dynamics of oppression . . . without giving way into despair and hopelessness about that condition."[2] The Framework offers four stages to help us consider the social context of our work as we move toward liberatory consciousness: Awareness, Analysis, Action, and Accountability. The steps work in a cyclical fashion; therefore, moving forward we refer to the diagram as the "Cycle." Each step serves as a reminder in our lives that the development and practice of a liberatory consciousness is dynamic and ongoing work.

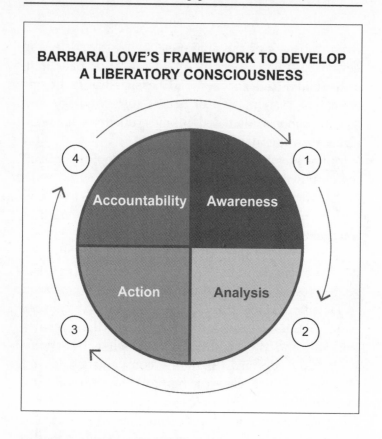

Awareness

The first step, *awareness*, involves "developing the capacity to notice, to give attention to our daily lives, our language, our behaviors, and even our thoughts." Noticing how injustice manifests in different areas of our life is the first step toward equity, and acknowledging that we are socialized to value some groups of people over others is key to this analysis. The chart below outlines identities that are categorized as "dominant" or "nondominant" groups; dominant groups often benefit from unearned privilege, whereas nondominant groups experience unearned disadvantages through lack of access to education, health care, and wealth, among other things. Reflecting on the process of filling out the checkboxes can help illuminate how these categories are socially constructed, arbitrary, and unjust.

SOCIAL CONSTRUCTIONS OF IDENTITIES

Dominant:

☐ White

☐ Able-bodied

☐ Heterosexual

☐ Cisgender
(Identify with the gender assigned at birth)

☐ Male

☐ Adult

☐ Middle or owning class

☐ Light skinned

☐ English speaking

☐ Citizenship

☐ College Educated

☐ Christian

Nondominant:

☐ Nonwhite

☐ Disabled

☐ LGBTQ+
(Lesbian. Gay, Bisexual, Transgender, Queer, Intersex+)

☐ Female

☐ Children/Youth/Elder

☐ Poor or working class

☐ Darker skinned

☐ Not English speaking

☐ Immigrant

☐ Undocumented

☐ Incarcerated or formerly incarcerated

☐ Sex worker

☐ Non-Christian

We must remember that these categories are not natural and are socially constructed. These are *systems of oppression* that are linked to these identities; for example, *racism* is a system that assigns more value to people who appear to be of European descent. Even more disturbing is the fact that those who are marginalized can experience *internalized oppression*, which occurs when a person of color, for

23

example, comes to believe that they are inferior to white people. Those in dominant groups may come to experience *internalized domination*; for example, a daughter who gets her PhD might come to believe that she is more valuable than her mother because of her educational pedigree.

One way to become aware of inequities is to fill out the chart and check off which categories you identify with. The point is not to simply dwell on (or feel guilty about) whether one has more check marks on the left or the right, but to simply notice in an objective manner that such categories exist. Also, many of us check off boxes on both dominant and nondominant categories because our identities are *intersectional*, which complicates how we experience the chart. Awareness includes noticing how one feels as we check these boxes off: are we affirmed? Surprised? Defensive? Once we understand that these categories do not define us, we can depersonalize the experiences of oppression. As adults committed to liberation, we make an intention to be attentive to individual, structural, and institutional factors that impact all of us, but most especially young people and their communities.

Analysis

Step 2 is *analysis*, the examination of why the world is as it is. To dismantle oppressive systems, a strong analysis *of individual, structural, and systemic changes that center the experience of those directly affected* is needed. In this step, one continues to ask questions about why systems of oppression exist. Take school policies that punish students who are Black for their hair as an example. One would ask questions about why administrators in certain schools feel that locs warrant punishment. We would examine historical associations with Black hair and how slavery and colonialism have impacted cultural framing of straight hair as superior to curly hair. Once we understand the factors of discriminatory discipline policies, we are prepared to act; we must be mindful to not get stuck in "analysis paralysis" by solely discussing problems in meetings or Circles. We must use power to create meaningful change.

Action

Step 3 is *action*, where one develops and puts into action strategies formulated from the analysis. One does not proceed to act without first considering one's own positionality and how to collaborate (or co-conspire) with others who are most impacted by injustice. At the same time this work is for *all* of us, not just for those in nondominant groups. In the analysis step, we realize that we have validity and power as individuals and groups, and understand the root causes of oppression. In the action step, we figure out what to do with this knowledge. Action is not necessarily about focusing on one particular problem. Instead, it is about dismantling oppressive ideologies and systems. In the example of administrators punishing Black students who wear their hair naturally, it would be a start to fight this singular rule, but a deeper commitment to ending the ideology that supports such a policy is necessary. In action we embrace and trust that youth are valuable holders of wisdom who offer solutions in the movement for liberation.

Accountability

Accountability is owning the responsibility to intentionally interrupt systems of oppression at all levels, starting with our own praxis. In this step, one consistently considers how to keep themselves accountable to fight racism, ageism, and other systems of oppression by being aware of how they utilize, leverage, or minimize their own power. One example of this involves dismantling adults' need to dominate spaces and Circle. If adults are invited on a panel to speak on restorative justice, they must be accountable to youth, and to themselves, to shift power dynamics by advocating that young people are invited to speak as well. In taking responsibility to question, explore, and challenge their socialized roles, those in dominant groups (i.e., adults) acknowledge and reflect on how to responsibly share and/or relinquish power, while those in nondominant groups (i.e., youth) acknowledge and reflect on how they are impacted by their socialization.

Love originally named this step "accountability/ally-ship," but the term *ally-ship*, once considered radical, can connote supporting those who struggle without having anything at stake. One cannot simply claim, "I am an ally." Allyship is earned and starts with listening, building community, and rising in solidarity—and humility—with others. Being an ally is an ongoing process as one unlearns the stereotypes and ideologies that prevent us from honoring every person in their full humanity. One can place a "Black Lives Matter" sign in their window or yard without engaging in further action to make systemic change, or without acknowledging that they have implicit bias against Black people despite their good intentions. The work of "accountability" is to be in community with people who challenge one another to unlearn oppressive systems of thought. In this step of the Cycle people in dominant and nondominant groups hold systems, themselves, and each other accountable because they understand, ultimately, that their liberation is intertwined.

Love's Cycle provides a framework to deepen our analysis of the school context in which youth engagement occurs and live out restorative principles and the core value of liberatory education. As we work in authentic intergenerational partnerships in restorative justice in education, we must also model actions that lead to justice and equity.

The Liberatory Consciousness Cycle: Reflection Questions

When engaging with the Cycle, adult and youth RJ practitioners can answer these questions together to deepen praxis and collaborate to build equitable schools.

Awareness
- How do my identities impact how I think, act, or relate to others?
- What categories do stakeholders in the community identify with? Are these identities valued and embraced in schools?
- What do I know about the historical and lived experiences of people pushed to the margins?

(Continued on next page)

- How do I partner with youth and adults?
- What do I notice about who is in power and who is valued in schools?

Analysis

- Why do certain groups have power over others in schools?
- What perspectives (besides my own) need to be considered when analyzing an issue?
- Am I aware of my own biases?
- What do I need to learn?
- What are the roots of my current way of thinking?

Action

- Am I the person that needs to take action? How can I support or partner with others to take action?
- How can we support a younger person to have agency?
- How can we leverage resources to support youth?
- How am I going to move forward the next time I encounter an unjust situation?

Accountability

- How can I be vulnerable even with my fears and frustrations?
- How will I intentionally and continuously work to check my own privilege and power as an adult working with youth or as a youth working with adults?
- How can I be authentic and honest as I keep myself and others accountable?

Chapter 4
Laying the Foundation for Work with Youth: Anti-Adultism

I recently co-facilitated a training on restorative practices. Although I knew how to lead a Circle, I never had outside of school or without Dr. Wadhwa's [my teacher's] input. It felt strange that during the preparation, I was genuinely asked for my input. The process felt different, as I wasn't regarded as someone else's mentee, but as a person who knew what she was doing. Without realizing it, the power dynamic between me and Dr. Wadhwa made me doubt my skills. That sense of independence increased my confidence, as I realized that not just other people could believe in me, but that I could as well. —Mirna Benavente, Houston

In this anecdote, Mirna Benavente, currently a high school senior and lead teaching assistant in a restorative justice class, reflects on how she did not see herself as someone with expertise in restorative justice until invited into a space outside school. Though Anita Wadhwa partnered with youth and trusted them as classroom teachers, she learned that her mere presence as an authority figure nonetheless placed a constraint on Mirna.

Mirna's story is illustrative of the ongoing need for all adults who work with youth to continually re-examine how they may be operating from an "adult-ist" lens. Being in right relationships includes being in equitable relationships, where there is care and responsibility and not hurt. It is for this reason that doing any intergenerational work in restorative justice requires a deep understanding of "adultism" and the myriad ways it manifests itself even within the most experienced and well-intentioned youth advocates.

Simply put, adultism is the inherent and structural bias of adults against youth.[1] Adultism emerges when a dominant group exercises power over a subordinate group, in this case adults over young people. We affirm Fletcher's statement that *all adults are adultist* and propose that those who want to work with youth should be actively "anti-adultist." Acknowledging that all adults are adultist helps us move beyond paternalism to truly liberatory pedagogy.

In this chapter, we offer examples of adultism in RJ work at both the interpersonal and structural levels. We then utilize the Cycle as a tool to show how adults and older youth can continuously counter their adultist tendencies.

Adultism at the Interpersonal and Institutional Levels

Adultism at the *interpersonal level* occurs when some-one puts a younger person down or minimizes their value in their speech or actions. Examples of adultism can include implementation of Circles that are always adult led; adult domination of the talking piece and Circle space; and forcing students to participate in Circle for a grade. Building on Fletcher's everyday examples of adultism,[2] in schools we often hear,

"You are so articulate for a middle school student."

"Don't yell in my classroom!" (while yelling)

"Wow! Where did you learn to hold a circle *LIKE THAT?*"

"Who is the adult in charge of facilitating the Circle with youth?"

"I think an adult should handle this."

"You're just a kid."

"You should know this by now."

"You'll understand when you're older [or have more life experience]:"

Youth may experience these phrases as oppressive, and yet when they work with students younger than them, they can also mimic and display adultist behaviors by presuming that those younger than them lack capacity, understanding, or innovative ideas.

Adultism also occurs at the *institutional* level. Schools can be a petri dish for adultism, as they are often built on policies, laws, and programs that rarely engage young people as partners in their creation, but are "done to" young people. Well-meaning adults, for example, craft policies like curfews to keep youth safe; however, "doing for" young people undermines youth as part of the solution and inhibits effectiveness and authentic engagement.

Students hold both critical perspectives and solutions to the issues they face. However, they are often not invited to brainstorm possibilities, nor confer with the final policies implemented. Institutional adultism is at play when youth representatives on school boards serve only in a nonvoting advisory role. In addition, youth are rarely eligible to elect school board members; therefore, those most impacted have no direct representation in school districts.

Utilizing the Cycle to Counter Adultism

To disrupt adultist structures at the interpersonal level, in classrooms, and at the institutional level, RJ practitioners can engage in Barbara Love's Cycle. In the following example, we engage in the four steps of the Cycle to model how the reflective cycle can continuously challenge adults to undo their adultism, starting with examples of micro-interactions between a teacher and young people.

Interpersonal Adultism: Anita's Journal Entry
There's a trick that new teachers are taught to use on the first day of school. Let your students "choose" the rules collectively, and the list they produce will ultimately mimic what you, the adult, would have listed anyway. However, this trick allows you to create "buy-in" so students behave more respectfully. After all—they created the rules!

I started my career in 2001 teaching 9th-grade English using this tactic. I thought I was engaging with youth. In reality, I was trying to promote youth obedience to my ultimate structure and expectations.

Step 1 toward Anti-Adultism: Awareness

A primary step in creating awareness of adultism is to deconstruct the messages, biases, and narratives around control and obedience that most of us internalized in childhood. The question is *how* does one become aware of those things that are by nature implicit and often unconscious? Above, Anita teased out her history of adultism through a written reflection because she was asked to reflect on her classroom procedures in a graduate course on equity. Writing about one's work on a continuous basis provides space to uncover moments of adultism.

Others may turn to reflective practices such as meditation, immersion in nature, therapy, somatic work, and Circle with other practitioners to uncover moments of adultism in their work with younger people. The call to reflection can be deeply unsettling and painful. For healing to begin, developing praxis—an ongoing reflective practice—is key.

Reflective Practice Journaling Prompts

Youth and adult restorative justice practitioners can journal on the following questions to build ongoing awareness around adultism:

- When is a time you felt mistreated and oppressed by someone older because of your age? How did it make you feel?
- Have you ever behaved in a similarly oppressive way to someone younger than yourself? If so, in what ways? How did it make you feel?

[Continued on next page]

- Have you ever had a power struggle with a younger person and kept fighting because you needed to be "right"? If so, where do you think that feeling came from? Where did you get the messaging that adults need to be right?
- What behaviors of younger people, if any, trigger negative emotions in you? Where do you think that feeling comes from?

Step 2 toward Anti-Adultism: Analysis

In step 2 of the Cycle, Anita analyzed why she chose a process to create class agreements that ultimately were meant to privilege adult-created norms. In the analysis stage, adults attempt to connect interactions with youth to larger injustices, including the history of oppression in this country. In graduate school, Anita was exposed to readings that taught her how to have a critical analysis of the power dynamics between teachers and students. She wondered whether part of her adultism stemmed from structures around discipline and control that began 500 years ago, from the times of slavery[3] to American Indian boarding schools and the disproportionate suspending and expelling of Black, Indigenous, and Latinx youth.

Step 3 toward Anti-Adultism: Action

To give life to the core value of intergenerational partnerships, action involves partnership *with* young people, not *to* or *for*. Anita committed herself to working with youth to disrupt patterns of how teachers spoke to students or how assistant principals doled out discipline. She offered Circle as a space where youth could air grievances and solutions to injustices related to arbitrary rules (for example, boys who did not shave were sent to in-school suspension) that limit their educational opportunities. Later in her career, this led to the cocreation of a youth-led restorative justice leadership model where students train community members in Circle and restorative justice practices.

Step 4 toward Anti-Adultism: Accountability

In keeping herself accountable to being anti-adultist, Anita began reading books on how teachers could regularly engage in praxis alongside youth. Small groups of students volunteered to meet for pizza to provide feedback on how to improve the class and make it more culturally relevant. They continued to meet for the duration of the year so they could collectively develop the class, keeping their shared goals in mind.

The Complexity of Adultism: When Is it Okay for Adults to Have More Power?

We caution against binary notions of what is adultist or not adultist. We are cognizant that young people benefit from the power adults can leverage, and the wisdom and guidance of elders should not, in our estimation, be devalued. We embrace multifaceted indigenous cultural teachings in which elders are often given reverence and power simply by virtue of their age, and children and young people are also valued as members of the community.

We hold the tension that young people should be at the table to make important decisions regarding their lives and schooling, understanding that young people are still developing and have evolving capacities to make decisions and have age-appropriate agency in their lives.[4] The dynamic notion of evolving capacities reminds us that we can hold a growth mindset and that for young people to participate we must be aware of their individual, cultural, social, and educational needs. Youth yearn for structures and support in which they can grow and thrive. Adults must seek balance between supporting young people's development and growth while honoring their agency and providing them the guidance and respect they deserve. Adults have the responsibility and opportunity to acknowledge and leverage their adult power. Youth and adults are invited to lean into discomfort—where the growth happens—so that we continue to be intentional in sharing power across generations.

Chapter 5
A Typology of Youth Engagement in Restorative Justice

Young people make up the majority of a school's population and have vital perspectives on how to create equitable learning environments, but they are rarely part of key decisions that affect their lives. They, especially those pushed to the margins, must be at the center as decision-makers.

There are various modalities for engaging youth in restorative justice. Taken together, these modalities offer a typology for youth engagement. In the next three chapters, we provide examples of these modalities from Houston, Holyoke, and Oakland, and offer tips collectively created by adults and youth to guide practitioners in the work.

Youth Engagement in Restorative Justice	
Modalities	**Description**
Youth as Circle Keepers	Youth design and keep Circles in and outside schools.
Youth as Educators	Youth create curriculum and teach peers in an RJ class or unit. Youth train and coach both young people and adults in restorative justice and Circle processes.
Youth as Decision Makers	Youth serve on decision-making bodies, including committees and boards, and make decisions about policies and practices in schools and the district as voting and nonvoting members. Youth write policies at the school, district, local, and statewide level.
Youth as Researchers and Evaluators	Youth learn research methods, collectively identify problems that impact their communities, and engage in research to come up with recommendations or changes to redress the issues, including structural ones. Youth evaluate the programs, organizations, and systems designed to serve them.
Youth as Organizers	Youth strategize and advocate for social change by defining issues using research and political analysis, building alliances and coalitions and engaging in direct action and political mobilization to shift power.
Youth as Staff	Students and alumni work as interns and/or fellows in an RJ leadership role to implement RJ at the site or district level. They are paid or get class credit for their work.

38

Chapter 6

"Education, Liberation!": Apprenticing Youth as Restorative Justice Teachers in Houston

by Anita Wadhwa

There are 20 young people seated on the floor in a sloppy Circle at the start of class, some with eyes closed, others laying down with heads propped up on backpacks between desks that have been pushed away. Angel, the teacher of the course and a senior about to graduate, leads 10th-, 11th-, and 12th-grade peers in meditation. *Don't think about your stress. Go to your happy place*, Angel intones.

When the mindful moment is over, Angel taps a large bronze singing bowl and runs the mallet around its rim, bathing the space with a high, yet somehow calming, pitch. Students shift and sit back up, returning groggily to the space, and snap in support of the meditation. The class is buzzing loudly with excitement as students talk to one another about the happenings of the day. Angel uses call-and-response to get their attention, yelling, "Education!" The students pause and yell back, "Liberation!" Angel hands the talking piece to another student, who starts: "Okay, let's check in. What color are you feeling today? I'll start . . ."

In my role as restorative justice coordinator at a high school in Houston, I introduced and taught an RJ course called Leadership. Calling out *education, liberation!* in our class provided a continual reminder that we work to rip down barriers within our Circles, the school, and all of society. Three years later, it became completely self-taught by students who had already taken the class.

I begin this chapter with the history of Leadership and the structure of the campus RJ program overall, which is rooted in the modalities of youth as trainers and youth as teachers. This chapter focuses more on the latter modality, paying special attention to the processes by which three youth RJ teachers— Angel Lagunas, Leslie Lux, and Beatriz Macareno Rodriguez—taught Leadership to a classroom of peers. I conclude with the difficulties that arise when youth RJ teachers are tasked with carrying on a schoolwide RJ program alone.

The School

Yes Prep Northbrook High School (YPNHS), part of YES Prep Public Schools, is a public charter school of 800 students in grades 9–12 who predominantly come from low-income backgrounds. About 98 percent of our students are Latinx, with families in Mexico and Central America. Many students are detribalized and unaware of their indigenous roots, and therefore do not identify as "Native American," though they do not see themselves as "Black," "White," or "Asian" either. Our school sits on land that originally belonged to the Akokisa, Atakapa-Ishak, Karankawa, and Sana peoples, among others.

We share a campus with a traditional larger public school, Northbrook High; the goal of this partnership was that we share resources and academic practices. However, the merging of the schools created friction due to the misalignment of our disciplinary structures; we were founded on the principles of RJ while Northbrook historically operates with a more punitive model of addressing behavior. Another misalignment was that we were focused on principles of social justice, which was anathema to many people with conservative views in the partnership. For example, we were asked to change one of our murals of a fist in the air because it was seen as too aggressive. We added a diploma to the fist to make it amenable to our counterparts.

Contrary to stereotypes of charter schools, we were not siphoning off a particular group of students from the partnership, which has over 1,500 students: we have many students with disabilities, English language learners, and a range of academic achievement. As in any other school, some of our students drop out to work for their families.

When I was hired in 2015 by school director and RJ advocate Bryan Reed, adult-led Circles were already embedded in the school. Professional development sessions began in Circle, teachers Circled up throughout the semester to support one another, and teachers regularly led Circles with students to build relationships. All 800 students on campus sit

41

in a 15-minute tier 1 community-building Circle at least once a week (9th-grade students Circle up a second time in the week to build strong foundational relationships since they are newest to campus). I was hired as an RJ coordinator to integrate systems for youth to lead alongside the movement to create a fully restorative school. I offered to teach an RJ Leadership course rooted in Circle practices and a curriculum that explored systems of oppression that impacted students, families, and educators.

The Leadership Class

Each year 20 students are selected by their peers to join Leadership, an RJ course where they learn how to become Circle keepers and study restorative justice, systems of oppression, identity, and self-care. These Leadership students are a blend of introverts and extroverts, students with high grades and low grades, those who have had behavioral issues and those who haven't. But there is only one requirement: that they have the emotional maturity and openness to push themselves out of their comfort zone and be able to keep Circles, hold confidential information, report incidents of harm, and receive feedback.

The learning is experiential; the teacher models the use of Circles daily and students then co-keep their own Circles with 9th graders once a week. Along the way they meet virtually with RJ practitioners who work in prisons, schools, and community groups, and train others around the city during field trips to local schools and institutions. They engage in leadership development through writing narratives about their life and practicing public speaking. Leadership students also write the 9th-grade Circle scripts on topics such as toxic masculinity, the value of family, the school-to-prison pipeline, and mental health.

The RJ Leadership Tracks: Youth as Trainers and Youth as Teachers

We call the student restorative justice program YAM, or Youth Apprenticeship Model. I chose the word *apprentice* because while you can pay for RJ training and receive professional certification as a facilitator, I did not truly learn how to keep Circles until I worked under the tutelage of experienced Circle keeper Janet Connors, who I observed for dozens of hours.[1] YAM offers two tracks for students interested in RJ on campus: a trainer track and a teacher track.

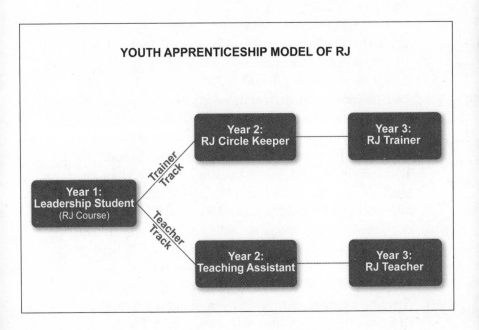

YOUTH APPRENTICESHIP MODEL OF RJ

Year 1: Leadership Student (RJ Course)

Trainer Track

Year 2: RJ Circle Keeper

Year 3: RJ Trainer

Teacher Track

Year 2: Teaching Assistant

Year 3: RJ Teacher

Trainer track

This track was developed when students in the first Leadership course pushed me to offer years 2 and 3 of the program. Leadership students can apply to be *RJ Circle Keepers* who work with me in the Peace Room to keep Circles for harm repair and more specialized circles for individual students for support, healing, accountability, and reentry from absences due to suspensions or any other reason. The Peace Room is a dimly lit classroom with a centerpiece, chairs in a Circle, and mindfulness stations with painting materials, stress balls, and books. RJ Circle Keepers can apply to be an *RJ Trainer* in year 3. RJ Trainers work in the Peace Room to apprentice RJ Circle Keepers.

Teacher Track

A Leadership student who wants to teach in year 2 of the YAM Track can apply to be one of four *teaching assistants* (TAs). In year 3 TAs can apply to become the *RJ teacher* in Leadership. This RJ teacher coaches TAs to write and deliver lessons, and supports students in the class with keeping Circles with their 9th graders. At the end of the year current RJ teachers interview TA candidates who want to teach; current TAs interview and select prospective TAs from the Leadership class; and Leadership students interview and choose the next Leadership cohort. Adults are not involved in choosing who is accepted in the program, though they can provide input. There is significant overlap between these two tracks. That is, RJ Trainers are still often co-keeping tier 2 and 3 Circles (for harm repair, re-entry, and support), and the RJ teacher and TAs also still keep tier 1 Circles (for community building) in Leadership every day. These roles are not discrete, but the titles are meant to distinguish between the skills built throughout YAM.

Development of the Teacher Track: A Social Experiment

In the original Leadership course, *I* led daily meditations and check-ins and crafted all the lessons. Students were "consulted" (a lower rung on the Ladder) on what topics they wanted to discuss, but I made ultimate decisions about curriculum, field trips, and grades. During my third year as RJ coordinator, Angel Lagunas (they/them), a student in the first-ever Leadership cohort, approached me with the idea of co-teaching the class. This seemed like a social experiment worth trying—if students could teach the course on their own, perhaps this model could be replicated elsewhere and create more student-led spaces in other YES Prep schools.

Leadership 2.0: Youth as TAs

Angel became Leadership's first Teaching Assistant (TA) in what I call *Leadership 2.0*. In 2.0, I was present only to take attendance, advising Angel on lessons and sitting at the back of the class—figuratively and physically removing myself from the Circle completely. Angel learned how to run a classroom logistically (e.g., transitioning between activities, encouraging student voice) through these experiences.

When I taught the class three years earlier, the first Leadership cohort had all been in 10th grade (the school was growing and had only two grade levels); now, we accepted 10th–12th graders in order to create a pipeline for the program. Angel remembers how the

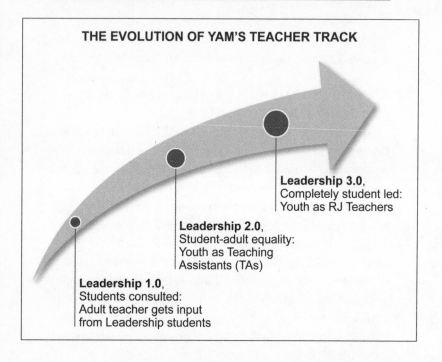

THE EVOLUTION OF YAM'S TEACHER TRACK

Leadership 3.0,
Completely student led:
Youth as RJ Teachers

Leadership 2.0,
Student-adult equality:
Youth as Teaching
Assistants (TAs)

Leadership 1.0,
Students consulted:
Adult teacher gets input
from Leadership students

intergenerational aspect of the course helped diminish the traditional teacher/student dynamic:

> [In class] I was like, "Yo let's get in Circle"—I would be saying it as the teacher. It was a sense of family and community—we're peers, right? A lot of times in high school there is a hierarchy like, "*Ew*, the freshmen, they're so annoying." Like we're better than them. But in Circle it was different. I just heard you talk about your family or that you have the same issue like me so we're kind of in the same boat here. There was a comradeship.

Because it was a social experiment, we learned by the end of the year that having only one young person take on a teaching role was a heavy responsibility. Angel revealed that they could have used more support in creating the curriculum:

> It was a little scary, for lack of a better word, but you've [Anita] always kind of thrown me into stuff since the beginning so it's just another day in the life. I could've used a little more support when some days I felt like I didn't know what I was doing and my peers could tell. So that was uncomfortable for me. I think we hadn't fully figured out what the lesson plans were . . . I remember we had a packet of readings in a binder. It was like a flexible syllabus.

Their comments remind me of the value that adult mentors have in apprenticing youth to teach. Though Angel could handle a lesson that was not "fully figured out," I could have positioned them to feel less fearful about lessons rather than "throwing them" into the spotlight. As a result of these challenges, Angel and I decided to have four TAs the following year, and one RJ teacher. The hope was that all five students could distribute the workload and support one another as they embarked on teaching.

Leadership 3.0: Completely Student Led
Angel selected Leslie Lux (she/her) to be the following year's RJ teacher because she was organized, reliable, and eager to teach a course that meant much to her personally. I now worked only half-time in the Peace Room, so I could not coach Leslie or the other TAs in real time. As the RJ teacher, she became overwhelmed with her full class load, applying to college,

and managing TAs who sometimes forgot to create lessons. She occasionally dropped by the Peace Room to see me for coaching. Says Leslie:

> You [Anita] would often just say you need to apprentice them [TAs] . . . they're not like you. I forget people are not on the same pace as I'm at. . . . You can't just give TAs feedback and leave it there. You have to provide some options and if those don't work, maybe you need to speak again and find what does work.

One of the TAs Leslie guided was Beatriz Macareno Rodriguez (she/her), who became the RJ teacher the following year during the pandemic. Since school was online, Beatriz had to learn how to build community, write curriculum, and coach TAs virtually. And because we were not on campus, she could not drop by the Peace Room and ask me for help. Youth engagement with RJ now fell on the "completely student led" rung of the Ladder.

Despite the challenges of teaching and coaching through a computer screen, Beatriz has flourished from a self-proclaimed shy person to a leader who felt comfortable approaching our principal, Greg Little, once students returned to school in person. She was frustrated when Leadership students revealed that some teachers were canceling Circles or not taking them seriously. Greg praised her approach. "She gave me the *business*," he told me, laughing. "But she was respectful and clear. She wanted to do professional development with teachers so they learned more about the importance of Circles, and we've set aside a day for her to do so." While Beatriz gained confidence

48

as the RJ teacher, she also felt untethered without the mentoring of a coach or an adult: "Whenever learning from Leslie [when I was a TA], I would get some advice and ways to improve myself. Now as an RJ teacher I don't have someone else to tell me what I can improve on."

Tips for Adults Working with RJ Teachers (and RJ Teachers Working with TAs)
• Provide a base curriculum that students can draw from to craft lessons.
• Schedule regular meetings to support lesson planning and ongoing evaluation of course and schoolwide Circles.
• Regularly touch base with RJ teacher (or TAs) about their well-being and provide resources for self-care (e.g., counseling, yoga, meditation)
• Periodically observe and provide feedback to TAs. Meet with RJ teachers to coach Leadership students in keeping Circles.
• Act as a bridge to support communication with teachers or administration.
• Coordinate guest speakers and other logistics for Leadership class.
• Publicize the work of RJ teachers during staff professional development to message the importance of this student-led initiative.
• Meet with alumni for inspiration and guidance.

Education, Liberation

Liberatory action and accountability must reside in what the oppressed group wants and needs.
—Angel Lagunas, RJ teacher

While youth RJ teachers flourish when they have autonomy to teach, they also need elders to support their learning and emotional well-being. My interviews with Angel, Leslie, and Beatriz revealed that they craved being in full partnership with a teacher or administrator who could help maximize the impact of restorative justice. When I asked Leslie whether Leadership provided a liberating space, she said, "Partially . . . liberation is being able to do things that can create a school wide impact, and we were limited on what actions we could do. . . . [Some] teachers who were not engaging in the practice limited the experience of students." Without an adult ally to leverage power to keep teachers "who were not engaging" in Circles accountable, it was hard for RJ teachers to feel valued for the work they put into prepping Leadership students, writing scripts, and coordinating logistics with staff.

The long-lasting impact of RJ teachers is also limited by a broader climate that does not support the full implementation of restorative justice. My school can only afford to hire me for RJ half-time. Our model has not infiltrated our partnership high school, where a new principal chose to get their administration trained in RJ from an outside entity rather than conferring with folks from our well-established program. Nor has YAM been implemented anywhere else in YES Prep, though the district is open to adopting restorative practices. Angel believes RJ work done for liberation must be done *with* "the oppressed group," but the Texas Education Agency refers to the philosophy as "restorative discipline," something to be done *to* young people.

The way Leslie, Angel, Beatriz, and other YAM graduates and I live out liberation is by working alongside one another to train community members in RJ work. We show up in Circles to check in with one another and share our celebrations and challenges. Over time they have begun calling me "Anita" without asking, and I find it endearing. In a few years, these YAM graduates will be teachers, social workers, lawyers, and organizers, and I trust that they will open doors for those who come after them. While our mantra of "education, liberation" may not have permeated our campus or district, these young people remind me that there is a difference between *schooling* and *education*: true education happens everywhere and in every moment, and in that sense, we are free.

Chapter 7
¡Sigue Pa'lante!: Collective Liberation in Holyoke
by Evelín Aquino

Es nuestro deber luchar por nuestra libertad.
Es nuestro deber luchar. Debemos amarnos y
apoyarnos. No tenemos nada que perder, solo
nuestras cadenas.

—Assata Shakur[1]

These words of love and community can be heard
at the closing of Circle as students chant them
in call-and-response style, one time in Spanish, then
three times in English, each time louder and with more
energy: "It is our duty to fight for our freedom. It is our
duty to win. We must love each other and support each
other. We have nothing to lose but our chains." These
powerful words of Shakur, a freedom fighter, activist,
and former Black Panther, convey the vision of liberation that is at the foundation of Pa'lante's work.

Pa'lante is a youth-led restorative and transformative justice program at Holyoke High School in Western Massachusetts, which sits on Pocomtuc and Nipmuc Land and has a student body that is over 80 percent Latinx. Pa'lante is a phrase made popular by the Young Lords, a group led by young activists of color, mostly Puerto Ricans, in the 60s that raised consciousness and fought to change inhumane conditions in their own urban communities. Pa'lante, the name of their newspaper, means "moving forward" and "reminds us that anything is possible when young people of color organize for change."[2]

In this chapter, the story of Pa'lante's journey reveals how a youth-led program, supported by an intergenerational advisory board, contributes to the development of youth as Circle keepers, researchers, and staff. This chapter focuses specifically on the modality of youth as researchers and on the involvement of youth fellows and alumni on a unique intergenerational board—opportunities that contribute toward community well-being and liberation.

This chapter is also personally meaningful as I (Evelín) am now assistant director of Pa'lante. I examine this work through the lens of a Puerto Rican/Dominican woman who grew up in the area and can identify with the students' lived experiences and realities, as they mirror my own.

The History of Holyoke and Pa'lante

Holyoke is home to one of the largest Puerto Rican communities outside the island, with a growing number of people from other Latin American countries calling it home. Holyoke has a history of being populated by a largely immigrant community recruited to

53

work in the local tobacco farms, which were similar to the sugarcane fields of Puerto Rico, through an initiative by the Department of Labor called the Farm Labor Program. Irish and Polish immigrants who have also lived in Holyoke for generations, but did not generally work in the fields, have assimilated and established themselves into the middle and upper classes of the community.[3]

The racialized opportunities for Irish immigrants, who became managers and bosses in the companies and factories that developed in the industrialized period of the city, created a strong division between the wealthier white Irish who "live up on the hill" and the predominantly working-class Puerto Ricans who live closer to the once bustling factories in the "Flats." During industrialization, many mills and factories were developed in Holyoke, in particular paper, giving the city its nickname "Paper City," and as farms began to close down, the mills and factories employed many of the laborers. As national industries moved overseas, the community was left with high unemployment, and poverty levels rose.

The socioeconomic and racial schism between different immigrant groups was reflected in an inequitable education system. Holyoke Public Schools developed a reputation for its below-average graduation rates, high suspension rates, and low standardized test scores, causing the state to take over.[4] With recommendations from Luke Woodward, the teen clinic therapist (housed in the school), students, and several teachers, the administration began to look for alternative approaches to supporting young people who received a high number of disciplinary referrals.

Together, after much research and data collection on the detrimental outcomes of traditional discipline and suspensions, they arrived at restorative justice as an approach they would explore.

The institutional racism embedded in the schools began to be viewed from a public health lens. Pa'lante became one of the few organizations in the city funded to work on addressing structural injustices in schools. After receiving a grant to create a youth-led restorative justice program, Pa'lante was born.

Observed Values of Pa'lante

Pa'lante harnesses the power of culture and community to name and address the harmful effects of structural policies that inhibit the well-being of the students and their families. Its specific mission is to "build youth power, center student voice, and organize for school discipline and educational policies and practices that actively dismantle the school to prison pipeline in Holyoke and beyond."[5] While the organization does not state the following as its core values, their work can be viewed through the following four goals, each symbolized in the main centerpiece used in Pa'lante Circles:

The centering of youth. Pa'lante's work is grounded in the priorities that youth themselves identify, such as unjust school and policing practices. Collective youth power is represented in the centerpiece with a statue of a group of children holding hands with a candle in the middle.

Transformation of self and community. As the students stand up for the issues that impact them, they are able to impact one another through the visibility of their representation and the work. The centerpiece includes a cloth made of an African fabric covered with butterflies, signifying the Indigenous roots of Circle, migration, and metamorphosis of self and community.

Liberation from oppressive systems. Youth who have been at the receiving end of discriminatory practices take a stand to claim their education and future livelihood. The centerpiece includes a copy of the Young Lords newspaper, named *Pa'lante*, and a book representing the Black Panther organization, connecting Pa'lante to the history of liberation movements and symbolizing how young people can use the media to educate and galvanize the community about issues negatively impacting their communities.

Community. The culture and work of Pa'lante is rooted in the Indigenous Circle process, which honors everyone's humanity, dignity, and sovereignty and is integral to all they do, from repairing harms to celebrating victories. The work is about restoring harmony within oneself and collectively as youth, community, educators, and elders work side by side. Pa'lante leaders have been taught by several Indigenous elders including Dr. Sayra Pinto, Harold and Phil Gatensby, Jose Lugo, and Rolf "Nohamm" Cachat-Schilling and Gwen Jones.

Modalities of Youth Engagement in RJ in Pa'lante

Pa'lante's restorative justice efforts involve three modalities with young people at the helm: peer leaders, youth participatory action research (YPAR), and youth as staff.[6]

Because the other case studies in this book discuss youth Circle Keepers in detail, I focus more on the ways peer leaders can deepen their engagement in RJ through YPAR and as members of a leadership pipeline in which they have the opportunity to be hired as alumni fellows. I then lift up a unique aspect of Pa'lante's organizational structure that has contributed to the sustainability of RJ work and youth leaders, their intergenerational advisory board, or CAB.

Developing Peer Leaders

Pa'lante honors the Indigenous roots of Circle and is intentional about avoiding co-optation of Circle practice to the extent possible with an institution. Pa'lante peer leaders attend a summer program that covers restorative justice, Circle, Ethnic Studies, political education, community building, and leadership skills. The majority of participants are Latinx, with several African American and white students. Administrators and teachers regularly call upon peer leaders to hold harm and healing Circles, and they also keep community-building and grieving and/or celebration Circles throughout Holyoke High School and in the organization.

Youth Participatory Action Research (YPAR)

Since its inception, Pa'lante has been committed to providing Peer Leaders the chance to engage in Youth Participatory Action Research (YPAR), a research methodology where the people being affected by injustice are not the "subjects" of research, but are the researchers themselves. Pa'lante was well supported in developing YPAR due to its close proximity to universities and relationships with scholars such as Antonio Nieves Martinez and Jerica Coffey. As an organizing tool, YPAR takes participants through an investigative data-collection process where they identify the issues and/or the root causes of issues and then work to formulate the action-based approach to challenge and transform the problem as they collectively see fit. Youth learn various research methodologies, including surveys, interviews, and storytelling, and include themselves, their peers, and communities as participants in the research, ensuring their perspectives are included in the data and findings. In the process, the findings are shared with all participants and the community at large so they gain a deeper understanding of the topics chosen by the youth to explore. Students take action to make changes based on their findings.

YPAR Example: Addressing Racism at Holyoke High School

One of Pa'lante's YPAR projects was a "racism audit" of Holyoke High School (HHS), through which youth explained how they experienced racism and analyzed possible strategies to make changes in their school. The Peer Leaders first articulated their *research questions*:

1. In what ways does racism operate at Holyoke High School?
2. How are different racial identities represented or not represented at Holyoke High School?

They then chose three *methodologies* to gather answers to these questions: schoolwide students were invited to fill out a survey during advisory; students were interviewed about their experiences; and pictures

58

were taken to document the ways different racial and ethnic groups were or were not represented throughout their school. They then *analyzed* what they heard and saw and summarized their analysis with four major *findings*:

1. Visuals in the building were mostly of white people and males.
2. Spanish-speaking students were mistreated and often told to speak English only.
3. Students of color were underrepresented in college prep courses and leadership positions in clubs.
4. Students were not exposed to a curriculum that addressed issues of race and racism.

After articulating the findings, the Peer Leaders made *recommendations* to address the findings. These included expanding Ethnic Studies for all students, strengthening relationships between students and predominantly white staff, promoting bilingualism, ensuring that there was more equitable representation in student organizations and college prep courses, and reflecting the student body throughout the walls of the school.

Specifically in response to the glaring absence of representation of the racial/ethnic, gender, and economic background of the majority of the student body, they set out to find out who were the heroes, the "Hidden Legends," who supported the well-being of the community, including those who identified as Latinx, Black, queer, and working class. They also sought community members they considered successful. Through interviews with and stories from the community and students, Pa'lante was able to identify leaders—both past and present—who had put their efforts toward making Holyoke a better place for the community. Pa'lante concluded their research with a community celebration honoring their Hidden Legends. In conjunction with the city and El Corazon Project, an initiative to create "a greater sense of belonging and cultural pride for residents of Holyoke,"[7] Pa'lante was able to put up flags or markers with pictures of the identified Legends along the vibrant Main Street of the Flats. Today, one can drive down the street and see the pictures and names of the many community members who have been instrumental in the growth and viability of the Holyoke community.

> **We also noticed that most of the pictures involving people of color showed them in subjugated positions—slavery or war internment camps. That is an important piece of history, but it isn't inspiring to students. It doesn't say to them that they can be up there one day, that they will do something great.**
> **—Katelyn, RJ alum**

In the 2020–2021 school year, the students partnered with the emerging Ethnic Studies department at HHS to campaign for a mandate to have all HHS students take Ethnic Studies as a graduation requirement. Pa'lante also addressed the inequity in the messaging of a sign which read, "No Hangeo" ("no loitering" in slang), a directive only meant for

Spanish speakers as there was no accompanying sign in English. After much deliberation with the administration, Pa'lante gathered and collectively, in the spirit of community, ceremoniously took down the sign and made the statement that we belong here and deserve recognition for our successes.

TIPS FOR WORKING WITH YOUTH IN YPAR:	TIPS FOR WORKING WITH ADULTS IN YPAR:
• Allow students to explore and voice their authentic concerns. • Teach an engaging YPAR process that introduces multiple research methods. • Maintain fidelity to youth voices by using their language. • Provide resources (food, printing, technology, etc.). • Support students by continuing to ask questions about their learnings. • Build in fun.	• Participate authentically and speak your truth. • Ask questions. • Step out of your comfort zone. • Take time to learn the research modalities. • Look to include all voices and perspectives in the research. • Be accountable, you are part of a team. • Allow yourself to be creative. • Build in fun.

Leadership Pipeline and Alumni Fellowship

Pa'lante has developed a school to leadership pipeline as a viable channel to employment for peer leader alumni through the fellowship program, and other staff positions. Pa'lante, committed to walking its talk by supporting leadership for the people, by the people, is building organizational capacity and systems for youth to be in leadership roles as staff. In the fellowship program alumni hold Circles throughout the school, coach a group of peer leaders, and give the younger students an opportunity to see themselves in leadership positions. The program also provides support in professional and personal development as fellows grow into their adult selves.

Pa'lante peer leaders and fellows have gained much acclaim in the Northeast as prominent leaders in RJ, providing training to youth and adults in restorative and transformative justice, Indigenous Circle process, and program development. Together they organize daylong events and speak on panels representing Pa'lante in the community.

Community Advisory Board

One of the most important mechanisms for Pa'lante is its intergenerational approach supporting youth-led programming, specifically through the Community Advisory Board (CAB). I enthusiastically joined the Pa'lante CAB in 2018. CAB consists of Pa'lante alumni, Pa'lante peer leaders' parents, city officials, activists, and educators who come together to support Pa'lante's work. Our positions and voices are used to leverage support for Pa'lante's work and youth-led research projects and/or to put a halt to the criminalization of students. CAB members are called to sign letters of support; show up and/or speak at school committee meetings; and mentor the students as they navigate through their high school experiences and on to their next chapters of higher education and life. CAB meets once a month to hear updates from the students, staff, and volunteers, share wisdom and resources, and to be in community. We hold Circle as our form of self-governance to nurture our relationships and interconnectedness.

Through the support of CAB, Pa'lante continues to flourish and work to transform systems that have historically been oppressive to the Latinx community and dismantle the school-to-prison pipeline at Holyoke High School and the community. By supporting the powerful leadership of the students and alumni, along with the adults who believe in them, they live out the power and principles of restorative justice and Indigenous Circle process.

Conclusion

Alumni fellows are sustaining the movement in Holyoke by taking on other leadership positions. A program alum now holds the full-time RJ coordinator position, coordinating the program's response to requests for Circles and coaching the peer leaders to prepare, keep, debrief, and follow up from Circles. Another Pa'lante alum has also been hired as the new CAB coordinator, working with Pa'lante's director and myself (the assistant director) to support the board's engagement and development.

In valuing culture and community, intergenerational partnerships demonstrate the unified front of the community addressing the issues they are most impacted by, as well as holding the youth in a Circle of support and trust as they lead us into a new reality of justice. Pa'lante builds together, researches together, organizes together, grieves together, heals together, celebrates together, and collectively moves toward liberation as a thriving community.

TIPS FOR DEVELOPING INTERGENERATIONAL ADVISORY BOARDS
• Recruit diverse community members committed to supporting RJ work, including program parents, business owners, school staff, community activists, donors, alumni, and peer leaders.
• Develop guidelines for members to understand the commitment.
• Schedule regular meetings.
• Meet at a central location in the community or a school.
• Maintain communication with members via email and/or social media.
• Make sure terms used in the meeting are accessible to all.
• Provide translation, if needed.
• Provide food and childcare, if needed.
• Provide updates about the program and its viability.
• Provide opportunities for members to engage with the program through events, presentations, committees, mentoring, etc.

Chapter 8

Nothing about Us without Us: Youth, Justice, and Unity in Oakland

by Itzamar Carmona Felipe and Heather Bligh Manchester

At the end-of-the-year RJ ceremony young people hand candles to their families showing appreciation for lighting their way. Promoting 5th and 8th grade students take the stage to receive talking pieces from older students who will support them at their next campus. Families and the RJ community stand in Circle around the graduates, symbolizing that it is our collective responsibility to dream, hold, and support each other.

Youth engagement in restorative justice in Oakland Unified School District (OUSD) began in 2011 at middle school sites. As middle school RJ leaders moved into high school and trained elementary school students in RJ practices with adult RJ Facilitators, they expanded the RJ ecosystem. Now, young people are Circle keepers, curriculum developers, trainers, teachers, peer leaders, representatives on decision-making bodies, policy writers, and organizers in and out of schools. Yearly, 450 Peer RJ Leaders from elementary through high school are trained, mentored, supported, and connected to an ever-expanding RJ network of alum and community members as they push for equitable schools. Youth, who often spend more time in OUSD than adults due to staff turnover, have been key catalysts for expanding restorative justice within the school district.

In this chapter, we explore the pivotal modalities that have transformed education through youth engagement in RJ: youth as staff, youth on decision-making bodies, and youth as organizers. We reveal that through these modalities, young people have infiltrated and shifted power in adult-led institutions and policies to build a collective liberatory consciousness. This chapter was written in collaboration with current OUSD students, alumni, and elders, and is based on our collective experience and involvement in Oakland and OUSD.[1] We sit in Circle on Ohlone people's land in unceded Huchiun territory and recognize that healing the harms caused by the genocide and continuous erasure of Indigenous Peoples is ongoing work we must do within and outside educational and other institutions. Representing over three generations of RJ practitioners working in our community, we begin with the movements that taught us

66

and laid the foundation for current youth engagement work in RJ.

Grounding in Movements that Came Before Us

The soil in Oakland has nourished generations of youth leaders, providing the environment for youth engagement in RJ to flourish. The birthplace of the Black Panther Party, Oakland is built on struggle, resistance, dreams, and alliance building. For over 60 years the Bay Area has been fertile ground for the fight for Ethnic Studies and the Asian Pacific Islander, Black Power, Chicano/Xicana, and American Indian Movements. Throughout the mid-1990s and early 2000s, young people joined together and organized against California laws that attempted to remove rights from undocumented immigrants, criminalize youth, and roll back affirmative action.

Circle practice was woven throughout the fabric of Oakland before it became known as the root of the restorative justice movement in schools. It was (and remains) a reclamation of communities' and students' ancestral knowledge. From the outset, students of color were at the forefront: Youth and community organizing in OUSD led to the creation of the Meaningful Student Engagement Department, which works to transform the school system to directly confront inequity and injustice.[2] The Department, a national model for community schools, incorporates the needs and cultural realities of students of color who are historically pushed to the margins of the education system, even in OUSD where they are a majority.

The community vision for RJ in Oakland combined with the roots of these movements prepared the soil for intergenerational partnerships to support youth as staff on decision-making bodies and as organizers.

Youth as Staff: Interns and Fellows

There were moments when I was a Circlekeeper teaching adults . . . it was intense, different. I have never been a leader like that. I did not realize that youth could be teachers to adults. We could both learn from each other, youth can learn from adults and adults from youth.

—Sandy Chales (she/her),
RJ Student Advisor, Alumni

In 2015, the RJ internship program for high school students and alumni emerged as the Restorative Justice Team explored ways to create structures and pathways to partner with youth on district-wide decision-making bodies and work with youth as co-trainers. Using the pre-existing academic and summer paid internship structures, youth were recruited. The internship program built concrete ways to share power including providing adequate workspace, creating business cards, and transforming the title of intern to RJ Student Advisor to give youth more power in adult-dominated spaces. RJ Student Advisors were trained and coached in restorative justice and joined the central staff, representing the voices of Peer RJ Leaders. Although every year the interns' focus looked different, they built on one another's work as they developed curricula and workshops.

This internship offered many students a springboard to expand their RJ work and connect to their cultures and communities. In the summer of 2017, Sandy Chales and Martha Calmo, RJ student advisors, strengthened the second iteration of the youth adult partnership workshop and tip sheet, adapted for the tips in this chapter.

Sandy and Martha held a community-building Circle for student leaders to get to know each other and create their shared values for the year. This was Yota Omo-Sowho's first Circle since moving from Nigeria to West Oakland. She reflected, "Navigating my new home and a new education system was incredibly challenging. But everything shifted the first time I sat in a restorative justice community-building Circle. It was my first time of feeling truly at peace in this country."[3] Now looking back, she shares:

> I was able to find something that connects to my family and story. . . . My ancestors and the ancestors of so many people sat in Circle before I came here. That wisdom guides me. Just knowing that is not just my story but knowing that my story is interconnected. . . . Circle strengthens that fiber. When I am in Circle I feel like my ancestors are guiding me.

Yota went on to be one of the strongest advocates for RJ in OUSD, a student advisor, and a coach for middle school RJ leaders, many of whom are now practitioners in high school and throughout Oakland. The Circle Sandy and Martha held created a ripple effect that supported generations of leaders that came after them. Years later, as alumni, Sandy and Yota returned to co-facilitate the first trilingual high school RJ training in Mam, Spanish, and English, ushering in a new wave of RJ leaders.

RJ Fellow Story
Itzamar Carmona Felipe (they/them)

An opportunity came up to partner with my middle school, Westlake, and teach a RJ class with Heather, the RJ program manager for youth engagement. Even though I loved working with middle school students, I did not feel very confident in my RJ training and overall facilitation skills. After each training, we would give each other feedback, debriefing about what worked and what should change. She would encourage me to take the risks, and through practice, I began to feel more comfortable as a facilitator and in my RJ training skills. Without the support and constant encouragement I wouldn't have been able to grow into my power. It was important to have someone see my potential, even when I was not able to see it for myself. I practice this with the high school students I work with today.

TIPS FOR ADULT WORKING WITH YOUTH AS STAFF:	TIPS FOR YOUTH WORKING WITH ADULT STAFF:
• Provide orientation and adequate training at the beginning of internship/ fellowship. • Provide a desk and necessary resources to be able to accomplish tasks. • Allocate time for regular check-ins with interns on the progression of their projects/tasks and see if they need support. • Listen to and ask for their ideas. • Be patient when they are learning a new skill or concept. • Meet with interns prior to and after meetings to go over the agenda and to provide time for clarifying questions.	• Be respectful and professional while being yourself. • Set boundaries by separating your personal and professional/work life. • Ensure that work is completed and that you are building relationships with the people you work with. • Ask questions and share your ideas.

RJ Youth Leaders on Decision-Making Bodies

Wherever decisions are being made that directly affect students and the student culture, RJ student leaders should be included.

—Maida Quintero (ella/she)
RJ student advisor, Alum

71

In OUSD, RJ student leaders bring a restorative lens and Circle practice to decision-making bodies at the school-site and district level. Within this modality there are distinctions among three types of decision-making bodies: *adult-dominated, youth-centered,* and *youth-led.*

RJ Youth Leaders on Adult-Dominated Decision-Making Bodies

Adult-dominated bodies are those with a majority number of adults and a few youth representatives. At the site-based level, RJ student leaders serve on Culture and Climate teams and the School Site Councils (SSC), a legal body of teachers, parents, administrators, and students who make site-based decisions around budget and improvement plans. As equitable voting members, RJ student leaders champion for sustainable funding and resources for restorative justice.

At the district level, two student directors, elected by their peers, serve on the adult-dominated OUSD Board of Education in an advisory capacity. The student directors represent 37,000 students and advocate for the students' priorities, including restorative justice initiatives. In 2015, RJ student advisors held

> **Being in SSC helped me learn and understand where the money is coming from and how it's being used. I had an amazing adult ally who helped me understand all the logistics and was there at every meeting to support me.**
> —Natalie Gallegos Chavez (she/her), RJ leader, LCAP student budget director[4]

the first Circle with the board of education, which seemed extraordinary at the time, but ultimately became normalized in Oakland. That same year, for example, the incoming mayor sat in Circles with 100 youth in her first 100 days in office. Six years later, three RJ student leaders have been elected to the OUSD Board of Education and continue to shift power as Circle practices influence meeting structures.

Youth-Centered Decision-Making Bodies

In *youth-centered* spaces, young people are the focus of the work while being consulted and engaged in specific design processes; however, they are not actively making decisions at every level. The Middle School All City Council (MSACC) is an intergenerational *youth-centered* district-wide middle school leadership body with youth and adult representatives, including peer RJ middle school leaders. Peer RJ middle school teams became known as leadership bodies on their campuses as they facilitated community-building, conflict, and healing circles in their schools and represented their peers on site-based decision-making bodies. MSACC convenes monthly to build leadership skills, develop networks, and support each other on site-based work while organizing the yearly Middle School Ethnic Studies Peer Leadership Conference. MSACC is facilitated by high school youth and adults, and while middle school students influence the creation of the conference and inform meeting structure, they are only able to do this within parameters that have already been established by adults. In other words, they do not decide if the conference is their collective focus for the year, as it has already been established that it will take place.

The middle school youth, however, design the theme, write the opening, and receive coaching to emcee the conference by high school and adult staff.

Nothing about us, without us: Youth, Justice, and Unity[5] was the youth-designed theme for the 2018 conference, reflecting the connections between RJ and Ethnic Studies. Restorative justice and Ethnic Studies are grounded in common principles such as building community and solidarity across groups, self-determination, and encouraging healing through listening and storytelling.[6] In her opening remarks, middle school student Teresa Sot invited her peers to create a united Oakland, where they could "come together, build relationships, break down barriers, connect, and be stronger together than as a single person." Following the youth-led opening, forty middle school peer RJ leaders held collectively designed Circles for 400 of their peers. Reflecting, Teresa shares,

It was not just a chance to grow together, but a chance to learn more about ourselves. I learned that it's okay to feel nervous as I was just getting used to my own skin. I remember connecting with other middle schoolers about what we strongly believe in. It's the first time where I felt that my opinions matter! Now as I lead a high school RJ team, keep Circles online, and colead RJ trainings I continue to build my confidence and skills.

Youth-Led Decision-Making Bodies

In *youth-led* spaces, young people choose the focus of the work while designing and facilitating the process and making decisions at all levels with guidance from adults. Strong *youth-led* spaces require a high level of adult support, ongoing coaching and training. The All City Council Student Union (ACCSU) is a high school *youth-led* district-wide governing body with youth, adults, and community organizations from 15 schools who work in OUSD "to create the necessary changes in Oakland schools that will benefit the students of Oakland, and the community."[7] They have an elected nine-member student governing board that meets weekly with two representatives on the board of education, plans and facilitates ACCSU meetings, and leads a yearly campaign, supported by the larger ACCSU. The governing board also receives coaching from adult staff and ongoing leadership training and development. ACCSU as a whole has been a strong advocate for RJ at the policy level, including passing a resolution to secure funding for restorative justice.[8]

By introducing Circle practice, student leaders developed a shared understanding of RJ that shifted the culture of the governing board. Former middle school RJ leaders, now in high school, began to infuse restorative justice practices into the governing structures of ACCSU including integrating Circle practice and values, providing RJ training for all governing board members, and transforming outdated elected positions such as changing the sergeant at arms position to the culture and climate director. The first student director of culture and climate was a former middle school peer RJ leader, whose responsibilities include incorporation of mindfulness and the

75

coordination of restorative justice practices to build community and address conflicts. These adaptations created a stronger sense of trust and community between the student leaders. Linh Le, former middle school RJ Leader and now ACC president, says, "Relational equity that is experienced in the ACC is not by mistake; restorative justice ensures that everyone is seen as a valuable equal, able to make contributions to the space."

Young people lead from their values and are not afraid to innovate and transform systems. In OUSD, hundreds of adults have been trained in RJ; however, it is the youth governing bodies that integrate RJ principles and practices into how they lead. Young people are applying restorative justice and transforming systems, giving adults an opportunity to reflect and explore ways we can lean into discomfort and lead in a new way.

TIPS FOR INTEGRATING YOUTH ON DECISION-MAKING BODIES:	TIPS FOR YOUTH ON DECISION-MAKING BODIES
• It is best to have two young people on a committee and a designated adult ally. • Build strong relationships with youth and ask for their thoughts and ideas. • Meet with youth prior to and after meetings to go over agenda, debrief, and strategize for future meetings.	• Be organized; have a place where you can keep track of your task/work for the week and month (i.e a planner). • Don't be afraid to ask questions and ask for help to make sure you understand what is happening. • Respect everyone in the space, adults and youth. • Be open-minded to new ideas from peers.

76

- Have an agenda that all can see and use facilitative methods where all can be heard.
- Have meaningful roles for youth during meetings (e.g., youth lead check-in questions, games, and other activities.)
- Schedule meetings when youth can attend, taking into consideration their schedules.
- Support youth in using calendar scheduling and email systems and listen to youths' ideas on new technology.
- Have former youth recruit and train new youth.
- Provide transportation, food, and stipends, and have fun!

- Connect with alumni or people that have been in your position before (they will be know what you are going through).
- Make relationships with adults and youth.
- Trust yourself! You are on this body for a reason and people want to know your thoughts.
- Have fun!

Youth Organizing for Restorative Justice

In response to looming budget cuts in 2018, students across the OUSD fought to keep restorative justice programs. The organizing strategy included youth participatory action research (YPAR), creating student budget priorities, alliance building across different groups, testifying at board meetings, initiating a social media campaign, and writing policy.

The ACCSU facilitated a research process in which they determined four budget priority areas, embedding restorative justice throughout: Student leadership programs, teacher quality, recruitment, retention and relationships, college and career support programs, and mental health, nutrition, and wellness.

Restorative justice student leaders, affiliated with ACCSU, built alliances with community and student organizations to amplify the student vision and called on these stakeholders to show their support at OUSD School Board meetings. Restorative justice leaders spoke at board meetings on the ways RJ had impacted their lives and demanded funding.

> To be a leader you have to make sure you are facing your own battles and coping with unsettling emotions. RJ is a great place for students to express and deal with emotions. The removal of RJ programs will affect students . . . they [will] have no one to talk to and the emotions will build up. . . . protect leadership programs, student engagement, and restorative justice.
> —Vida Mendoza (she/her), ACC leader

Youth who were not RJ student leaders but had been in Circles heard the call of their peers and stepped up, speaking to the ripple effect of restorative justice in the schools and community. RJ student advisor Griffen Castillo read from a stack of over 20 letters from his peers on the importance of funding RJ. One such letter from an Oakland Tech student stated, "Restorative Justice has allowed me to learn and understand what is going on in our country. . . . I don't want to live in a world where I am unable to listen and understand different sides of a story and find common ground. . . . If you understood what restorative justice could do for people, it would be the last program you consider cutting."

Students from Alliance Academy Middle School, with the support of their RJ facilitator, started a social media campaign with the hashtag #BelieveInRJ that spread throughout the district.

Despite months of organizing, the district announced that restorative justice funding, including foster care case managers and the Asian Pacific Islander Student Achievement (APISA) program, would be cut from the budget. This galvanized the students to develop a multipronged organizing strategy that reached beyond the school district. Students began to organize at the school, city, and county-wide level by speaking at meetings and convening in Circle with elected officials, including school board members, the city council, and county supervisors.

> Circle is not only about solving conflicts, it is about community building. . . . If you build a relationship with your mayor or principal, you can come back to that relationship. You are part of that community too, so you need to have that relationship and structure set; it makes students feel comfortable and welcome.
>
> —Linh Le (she/her), RJ advisor

By being in Circle with elected officials, RJ youth leaders built relationships with people in power and voiced their student budget priorities. Circle became an effective tool for organizing. By being in Circle with board members and the mayor, students began to gain an understanding of the interconnected political systems. In turn, through the Circle process, elected officials were able to see and hear young people, even if only for a small amount of time, as their equals.

In addition to Circles, youth partnered with a school board member to write and lobby for a policy[9] that would fund RJ and other priority areas. In a pivotal OUSD Board of Education meeting, Yota Omo-Sowho, the 2018–2019 student director, spoke on the influence of RJ and Circle in how she represents students:

> And I strongly believe giving young people the access to a quality education is truly what we need to shift these oppressive systems. . . . This is not just on a city level, it is about standing in solidarity with young girls around the world who are denied education, with children that are crossing the border as we speak, with young Black girls who are forced to grow up too fast, with the children in West Oakland who are able to recognize the sound of shots before they learn to read, with our "undocumented" immigrant community, with our LGBTQ community, with people who have been historically marginalized.[10]

Even though there was overwhelming support from students, staff, and community for the policy, it was lost by one vote. Although this was a setback, young people utilized their relationships, advocated at the city level, and secured one year of funding from the city of Oakland.

Going into the 2019–2020 school year, RJ in public schools was being defunded throughout California, so young people began to build at the state level, networking with the state superintendent of education and local officials. A Circle was planned with the state superintendent and the governor for spring of 2020, but when the pandemic hit, the organizing strategy shifted. As Circle went online, RJ youth and advocates simultaneously joined forces to support a local ballot initiative and campaign born out of the fight to save student services: Measure QQ led by the Oakland Youth Coalition. This ultimately passed through youth leadership within the Oakland Youth Vote Coalition, allowing 16- and 17-year-olds to vote for their OUSD School Board directors.

None of this work would have been possible if not for the legacies, collaboration, and dedication of Oakland-raised youth and elders who are grounded in their ancestral knowledge and continue to work in their community. It has been a long and tiresome fight, yet the work continues as middle school students enter high school and continue to advocate for funding, transform systems, and build unity through Circle at their schools and throughout Oakland.

TIPS FOR ADULTS in Youth Organizing	TIPS FOR YOUTH in Youth Organizing
• Support youth to understand and build coalitions and alliances. • Work across organizations and departments to build a strong web of alliances that support each other. • Meet with youth prior to and after meetings/ Circles to go over agenda; reflect, debrief, and strategize. • Provide adequate training on public speaking, political movements, system structures, etc. • Make language accessible for any and all youth. • When speaking at board and city council meetings, prep with youth in advance and provide transportation. • Model and integrate self and community care into the overall work.	• Practice speech when doing public comment or speaking in public. • Remember to breathe when feeling stressed or nervous. • Prepare ahead of time. • If you are confused, ask clarifying questions during prep. • Be willing to take risks and try new things. • Share knowledge of campaign with friends, peers, parents, and community. • Invite friends, peers, parents, and community members to events and actions.

Holding the Circle and the Fist

As young people organized to save RJ in 2018 and 2019 the image of holding both the Circle and the fist emerged. The fist in the air is a symbol with roots in the fight for Ethnic Studies, labor rights,

the American Indian Move-
ment (AIM), as well as the
Xicano, Asian Pacific Islander
and Black power movements.[11]
We created the Circle and the
Fist talking piece[12] to honor the
legacy of those who fought for
our rights before us and the
work we continue to do.

Embodying Fania Davis's
warrior-healer principle, where activism is social
healing and interpersonal healing is an act of justice,[13] students held Circle as a way to heal and shift
the education system, and marched to board meetings with their fist in the air, speaking their truth.
The fist claims space and power, connecting us to
our ancestors and past movements. It acknowledges
that we are not just sitting and talking about change,
but taking action: youth are reclaiming their rights
to a liberatory education by infiltrating adult-led governing structures and organizing for schooling that
values all students, so they are at the table and not
on the menu.[14]

Chapter 9

Youth Engagement in Restorative Justice: A Shifting Model of Leadership

written with Itzamar Carmona Felipe

Having a leadership role in a school activity is not the same as one in restorative justice . . . in student council, I asked myself what can I do for my grade level? While doing Circles I would ask myself, what can I do for my community?
—*Leslie Lux, RJ Alum, Houston*

Why be a star when you can make a constellation?
—*Naomi Murakawa*[1]

In K–12 education, the concept of leadership is often individualistic and linear, applicable only to the strongest public speakers and popular youth who are elected to hierarchical positions and entrusted with planning events and occasionally advising on school matters. These youth can be celebrated as "stars," rather than be encouraged to view themselves as part of a constellation. However, a new paradigm of leadership is emerging as youth transform the education system through restorative justice. The emergent leadership that restorative justice nourishes is communal, based in the whole and rooted in community, moving away from the "I" centric approach to the "we."

In interviews with restorative justice student leaders and alumni in our three regions, the common thread that ran through their experiences was the formation of their evolving identities as leaders. Over 30 RJ student leaders and alumni collectively contributed to the creation and vision of this chapter. Here we lift up their voices and metaphorically pass the talking piece so they may speak to the impact youth engagement in restorative justice has had on their lives and the core components of leadership that emerged from their experiences: deep listening, Circle keeping, agency, self and community care, accountability, and authentic community building.

Deep Listening

The root of communication, it is the ability to listen to self and others and speak one's truth with integrity

In Circle, the talking piece offers a tool that supports listening and gives everyone an opportunity to share their story. The talking piece invites one to sit with their emotions, not respond, and ground themselves by practicing the art of listening and being fully present. One can then transfer the discipline of the talking piece to their own lives, outside Circle. While listening with intentionality, one learns to read the Circle to what is said and not said and to hear the heartbeat and pulse of the community as one becomes more attuned to the world. Deep listening becomes a crucial skill in the development of not just how a young person presents in the world as a leader or organizer, but in how they are able to step into their own power.

It's weird how RJ has taught me how to listen [through] "one mic" [one person speaking at a time]—the talking piece is really helpful as emotions can get the best of you.
—Siurave Quintanilla Vasquez (she/her)

You learn to listen to the cues of Circle, how to interact with others and collaborate in and out of Circle.
—Jonathan Piper (he/him)

To really be a leader you have to listen. To everything. Listen to your community, to yourself, and the world around you. And all the answers that you need are there.
—Griffen Castillo (he/she/they)

Circle Keeping

The concrete skills and mindsets necessary to understand the ancestral wisdom of Circle, honor the humanity of one another, and practice empathy and patience to support and encourage peers, adults, friends, and family

In alignment with the sacred ancestral and Indigenous wisdom of holding Circles, students learn to prepare, with intentionality, to be in Circle with others. Through Circle, the student gains experience in preparing the space (e.g., the talking piece, centerpiece, placement of chairs) and crafting the agenda (e.g., the opening, community-building activities, rounds, and closing) to encourage connection and flow of stories. The practice of being in Circle goes beyond planning a physical Circle; it also involves learning how to hold authenticity and vulnerability, especially when young people hold Circle with their families. Circle keeping provides a deeper understanding of the value of honoring humanity in all aspects of their lives.

> *Being a Circle keeper supports the agency and autonomy of young people by trusting them to hold the Circle.*
> —*Itzamar Felipe Carmona (they/them)*

> *As we strip RJ of its layers, maybe we don't have a talking piece or are sitting in Circle, or we forget norms. But the basis is about sharing space and being a community. . . . It is about just holding space while eating or celebrating traditions—just sitting together.*
> —*Angel Lagunas (they/them)*

> *Moving traditional Circles online is just a part of exercising our muscle memory on keeping Circle. We need to adapt to change in order to be able to uphold these practices we value so much.*
> —*Ana Méndez (she/her)*

Agency

Capacity and confidence to speak from one's own truth, lead, hold space, and make one's own choices in and out of Circle

Youth involved in RJ gained an understanding of their own agency as they learned the skills needed to keep Circle, teach, and train others while advocating for change. Through being identified and supported as leaders, they gain confidence in their voices and feel whole in their identities. In being entrusted to design and keep Circles, they develop agency and power through encouragement by elders, and learn to navigate the world, more comfortable in their own skin.

I have a stuttering issue when I talk to people. Ms. [Tatiana] Chatterji [the RJ coordinator] recruited me to a Circle . . . and eventually I was leading the Circle. It was hard. I felt I was bad at it. They just said "you got this" [and] it got better. I was able to join other meetings, talk about my experiences and share how we can add RJ to other schools.

—*Dani Primous (she/her)*

The students think our school dynamic has changed for the better, because of the program. So, it's really important that it's not just some club that we're in, we are changing lives. And we're doing things that matter.

—*Pa'lante youth leader*

RJ has given me the voice, the power and strength that has pushed me to major in Poli Sci. It is important that those who have been impacted in negative ways move to upper levels to make the changes.

—*Sandy Chales (she/her)*

Self and Community Care

Focusing on the need to sustain community well-being by identifying and prioritizing the physical, emotional, spiritual, and mental health of self and others

Young people prioritize and advocate for mindfulness in Circles, meetings, and organizing spaces. This healing-centered approach prevalent today is a paradigm shift in youth engagement. Young people are advocating to be seen and see others, to slow down, find balance, and embrace laughter and fun. They understand that it is vital to be physically, emotionally, spiritually, and mentally healthy to thrive, because they see how past leaders have burned out. Youth acknowledge that ongoing Circles, regular check-ins with adults, and access to support services are needed to sustain their ability to do RJ work. The integration of self and community care in RJ supports students to balance the demands of life and education. Providing yoga, meditation, and online Circles during the COVID-19 pandemic in 2020–2021 offered time for youth to be vulnerable, heard, and held. Young people did not frame mindfulness practices as simple tactics for de-stressing; they saw them as essential to their individual and communal resilience, and freedom from oppressive structures.

Check-ins are important, like saying, "I value your work and you're good at it, but are you also okay with life and your family?" That's helpful, because family life and education impacts your work.

—Leslie Lux (she/her)

RJ is an incubator of resistance because it allows for the wisdom of community care to be at the forefront.

—Yota Omo-Sowho (she/her)

Accountability

Responsibility to self, community, those who came before us, and those who come after us

In honoring the wisdom of Circle and its origins, leaders are encouraged to be mindful of those who have come before in the work for justice and liberation. In taking responsibility for oneself, in and out of Circle, RJ leaders understand their work is connected to movements for harmony and just relationships. Young people learn to hold themselves accountable for their actions, in turn modeling for other young people and adults around them. Leaders, be they children, youth, adults, and elders, are called to walk their talk daily, understanding the importance of integrity and trust needed to truly manifest liberation.

Authentic community is not easily destroyed when it has deep roots fostered by people's vulnerability and willingness to practice accountability.
                              —Maida Quintero Medrano (ella/she)

You cannot be misogynistic and then come up into Leadership class and say, "let's talk about oppression." You're completely complicit. . . . Liberation is like saying "this is it." We're drawing the lines. [Sometimes I think] I need to be a little more open-hearted to allow people time to grow. Other times it's like nope, you had enough growing.

                              —Angel Lagunas (they/them)

One thing that's important is that this is not a way to avoid consequences. One of the key precepts of the program is facing your peers and having to own your own behavior, how to make amends. . . . For teens, that can be a more impactful consequence.

                              —Pa'lante Youth Leader

90

Authentic Community Building

Occurs when there is a space of trust where young people and adults can be vulnerable, share their authentic selves, and are seen and embraced in their full identities

Young people repeated the word "vulnerability" as a necessary component to do RJ work for both adults and youth. Alumni reflected that groups they were in after high school that did not build an authentic community struggled to reach their full potential. RJ leaders understood vulnerability is part of developing social emotional skills and a prerequisite to working deeply with others.

To connect across differences and commonality starts with an understanding of our own authentic selves. Students repeatedly explained an internal shift when they were able to sit in spaces where their holistic identities and lineages were acknowledged and honored. From this place, youth bring their whole selves to the Circle, challenging the dominant narrative of whose stories matter.

In Circle you learn to be vulnerable and how to connect with others through sharing your story.
—Juan Guillermo Pablo Matías (he/him/his)

As a young person I wanted people who would acknowledge me—especially because I didn't have that at home—to acknowledge the different parts of who I was. I was not just a good student, or not just undocumented, or not just queer, I was all of it.
—Itzamar Carmona Felipe (they/them)

I found RJ sacred, it's bringing the community together, making sure everyone and everything is included—people, water, the elements. This refers back to my Guatemalan culture—giving thanks to life and water and everything. This was something I was missing [from school].
—Martha Calmo (she/her)

91

Expanding the Constellation

The impact of restorative justice leadership in young people's lives is a vital catalyst for individual and systemic transformation. Juan Guillermo Pablo Matías, an RJ leader from Fremont High School in Oakland, embodies this shift in

> **RJ is the way my people can feel included.**
> **—Juan Guillermo Pablo Matías**

leadership. Juan, along with other multilingual RJ leaders, held Circles in their native languages as part of intentionally connecting newcomer students to the school community. Reflecting on the Circles he held in the Indigenous Guatemalan language, Mam, he says:

I have not seen Mam Circles in other schools. So many people lose culture and language because it's weird in a different country. They feel embarrassed. When I got here, I was a shy person and scared. I didn't have anybody to talk to or be connected with.

Bringing Guatemalan students who speak Mam into Circle was special and it was hard. Students needed it, they needed to share stories and see each other and they were coming with different problems and points of view. They really loved it. It was like we were in Guatemala. RJ is the way my people can feel included.

Immigrant and refugee youth were able to deepen their sense of belonging in school and in Oakland, while also feeling cultural pride and visibility. Juan applied these powerful experiences to a trilingual RJ

92

training in English, Spanish, and Mam at a neighboring school in East Oakland. The training planted seeds for authentic community between the Black, Chicano, and newcomer student participants.

Through their integration of honoring ancestral wisdom, taking care of self and community, and growing into their own leadership, young people are building capacity to live out restorative principles and sustain the movement by passing on their knowledge to those who come after them. In gaining Circle competencies, young people like Juan are vital partners in building schools that are just and equitable, and building authentic connections so that all young people feel seen.

(Continued on next page)

Components of Leadership in Restorative Justice[2]

Core Component	Talking Piece	Significance of Talking Piece
Deep listening		The conch shell awakens us to pay attention. It elicits positive vibrations, allowing for deep listening with all those called together.
Circle Keeping		Quetzalcoatl represents the knowledge all who sit in Circle hold and share. The Sankofa bird represents looking to the past, honoring the ancestral wisdom of Circle, and simultaneously looking forward, allowing ourselves to dream of liberated futures.[3]
Agency		The Circle and Fist represent the balance of interpersonal healing and connection along with taking a stand and acting with agency.
Self and Community Care		The lotus is a beautiful flower that emerges from the mud, indicating the possibility of beauty and multilayered well-being despite experiences of struggle.
Accountability		The sunflower removes toxins from the soil. The toxins are harms committed, and accountability is the sunflower that supports healing.
Authentic Community Building		The grove of redwoods represents a community that supports one another's growth. Redwoods share resources between roots, protecting one another from disease and harm.

Chapter 10
The Spiral: An Emerging Framework for Youth Engagement in Restorative Justice

RJ creates a powerful community. It builds unity, a genuine unity that allows us to engage in radical systemic change.

> —*Maida Quintero Medrano,*
> *RJ Leader and OUSD Alumni*

The young people involved in RJ in Oakland, Holyoke, and Houston all echoed Maida's sentiment that RJ builds an authentic community, but also has the capacity to create individual and systemic change. In this chapter, we suggest that by combining two of the theoretical lenses that ground this book—Fletcher's Ladder and Love's Cycle—youth and adults can collectively engage in praxis to create systemic change.

The Ladder offers a lens to develop an awareness of adultism and explore how to move beyond youth being tokenized. The Cycle offers a way to contextualize adultism and deepen the praxis by which to move toward intergenerational equity and ultimately liberation. In order to combine elements of the Ladder with the critical stages of the Cycle, we offer an emerging lens: the Youth Engagement Spiral.

The Youth Engagement Spiral

The Youth Engagement Spiral (henceforth referred to as the "Spiral") is dynamic because the Ladder and Cycle are intertwined; each coil represents a different rung from the Ladder in which one engages in the four stages of the Cycle. Unlike the Ladder, which has an end point of youth-adult equity, the Spiral ultimately moves beyond youth-adult equity to liberation. Similar to the way spirals hold stretch and hold tension, we must stretch beyond our comfort levels to fully engage and share power with each other as youth and adults, and constantly reflect on where our actions lie in the Spiral. Below, we offer a realistic, but hypothetical, scenario of how one RJ coordinator engages with the Spiral.

The Spiral in Action

Ms. Garcia has been a restorative justice coordinator at Palmer Elementary School for two years. She holds community-building Circles in the three 4th-grade classrooms once a week. She writes weekly Circle agendas based on student ideas for Circle topics. Ms. Garcia notices that in some classes students barely speak or pay attention in Circle, but when students volunteer to help her keep Circle, the class seems

96

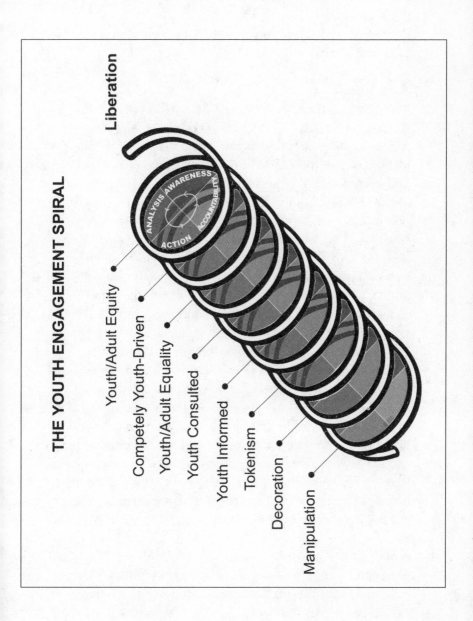

THE YOUTH ENGAGEMENT SPIRAL

Liberation

Youth/Adult Equity

Competely Youth-Driven

Youth/Adult Equality

Youth Consulted

Youth Informed

Tokenism

Decoration

Manipulation

ANALYSIS · AWARENESS · ACCOUNTABILITY · ACTION

more engaged. This dichotomy spurs her to pull out the Spiral and reflect on how to strengthen intergenerational partnerships in Circle.

Awareness

Ms. Garcia reflects on how she designed and kept the Circles. She looks at the Spiral and reflects, *how have I partnered with the students and 4th-grade teachers?* She identifies that the Circles are at "Students Consulted" and considers how she can move along the Spiral to "Student-Adult Equity" by starting with the first step, Awareness. She wonders, *How do my identities impact how I think, act, or relate to others? How do I navigate being assigned to these categories when working with members of a school community?* She reflects on being young, female, Latina, and light skinned in a school where the majority of teachers are White and female and are a mix of veteran and first-year teachers. The students mostly identify as Latino/a and are from working-class backgrounds, with a sizable population of English Language Learners. She asks herself, *What do I notice about who is in power in the classroom? Who is given value?* Many teachers run hierarchical classrooms, the school literature that is sent home is not translated in Spanish, and she has only seen one class where there are posters on the wall that look like the students. Since she first entered campus, she has heard rumblings about "this restorative justice fluff" and has felt defensive about her role.

Analysis

She realizes that her own preoccupation with how she is seen among the staff has prevented her from creating a system by which young people can own the Circle process. *Where does this preoccupation come from?*

98

She experiences discomfort as she realizes that she has tried to prove herself to white teachers, professors, and employers her entire life. Also, as a white Latina, she wonders if she has any internalized racism against her students, many of whom are darker skinned; is she discounting their ability to keep Circles with her? In this situation, she understands that she holds power in Circle simply by virtue of being an adult, and that her adultism is holding her back from allowing young people to keep Circles; she is also replicating the adultism that veteran teachers are displaying when they dismiss her capabilities due to her younger age. *What perspectives (besides my own) need to be considered?* She wonders what the students are thinking about the Circles and their experiences in the school and neighborhood. She reflects on whether the students feel their ideas and identities are valued. She realizes she has never asked them or involved them in designing a Circle. She also reflects on why she always has to lead and whether she truly trusts the students.

Action

Ms. Garcia asks herself, *Am I the person who needs to take action?* She decides that in order to be an anti-adultist, she must partner with students to figure out how to improve Circles. *How do I support others to take action?* She plans a Circle to ask the students what they notice is different when she keeps Circles versus when they volunteer to co-keep them.

She then reflects, *How can I as an adult leverage resources to support the students?* She asks teachers whether she can pull student volunteers from class and coach them in Circle planning and keeping. She then asks the principal whether she can replace

99

her 45-minute hallway duty once a week for these pullouts. She begins to meet with students regularly and supports them to keep Circles. As they build relationships, the students share about their families, cultures, and community. They choose to do a series of Circles about their families and home culture.

Accountability

Ms. Garcia recognizes her attempts at becoming an anti-adultist are ongoing and wonders, *How will I intentionally and continuously work to check my own privilege and power as an adult working with youth?* She is particularly concerned about her privilege as an English-speaking educator working with families whose home language is often Spanish. The students and Ms. Garcia craft a Circle agenda for a Family Circle Night, where parents, guardians, and siblings will be invited to learn about Circle and to discuss what they value in education for their families.

She reflects, *How can I lovingly witness the vulnerability, authenticity, and honesty of myself as I keep myself and others accountable?* She communicates with the staff and administration her learnings from the Spiral and acknowledges that students who kept Circle increased engagement among their peers. Ms. Garcia proposes to the administration that students co-keep Circles throughout the school. She invites administration, teachers, parents, and other students to learn to keep Circles, with students as co-trainers.

From Youth-Adult Equity to Liberation

Like the Ladder, the Spiral is sure to have limitations, but we offer this image as a tool to strengthen intergenerational partnership and liberatory education work in restorative justice in schools. To reiterate, the outcome of the Spiral is to move toward liberation. This means honoring each member of the community's experience and knowledge at all stages of life and working side by side to create the world they envision, toward the greater goal of ending structural injustice. RJ work would result in a society that does not sort people as valuable or disposable based on their identity roles. Though liberation may never come to fruition, it is an ongoing goal—elusive and ethereal—and one that can push young people and adults to fight for just and equitable schools.

Chapter 11

Intergenerational Partnerships for Liberation: A Call to Action

In these times of social eruption and revolution, young people are taking a stand and modeling an emergent form of leadership that holds the Circle and the Fist. In shifting the culture of power around who is seen as valuable, young people are naming injustice and demanding change. Youth and adults together hold the opportunity to build a collective movement. It is a time to share power and honor the wisdom of all members of the community as we work to reimagine education.

We wrote this book during the COVID-19 pandemic, which manifested unprecedented opportunities for the cross-pollination of justice work; thousands of people across racial lines masked up to support the Black Lives Matter movement, advocate for immigrant and transgender rights, and demand action for climate change. Activism extended into virtual spaces as inequities were exposed and exacerbated. RJ practitioners organized mutual aid; young people assisted elders with technology, schools provided rental assistance, and intergenerational teams organized online forums addressing health and school concerns. To hold and support one another, students and adults across the country held Circles online, building resilience in a time when hundreds of thousands were dying from a pandemic, families lost their livelihoods, and Black people continued to die at the hands of police. Young people infiltrated traditionally adult dominated spaces: they were keynote speakers at RJ convenings on the importance of organizing for systemic change, and spoke at board meetings demanding the removal of policing from schools.

As a call to action to maintain this momentum, we invite readers to reimagine how power is distributed in schools and offer the following recommendations—created jointly with the youth from our three cities—for RJ practitioners working intergenerationally for justice and equity.

- **Honor all cultures and indigenous traditions, including your own, those of students and communities, and those of the people who originally inhabited the land.**
  Learn about the Indigenous people who originally inhabited the land where you reside. Be mindful of appropriating Indigenous practices, and find out what role you can play to support/amplify the communities who still live with the consequences of the First Harm (genocide of Indigenous peoples).[1] Research and share your own cultural traditions

and support others to share and integrate their own in Circle.

• **Demand that young people are partners in any decision that impacts their lives and their communities.**
It is all of our responsibility to shift power so that young people represent themselves and make decisions that affect their lives. Advocate that young people are present and have power in any space where you (as an adult or young person engaged in RJ) are invited to speak on or make policies around restorative justice.

• **Youth, trust yourselves and your innate wisdom. Adults, trust youth and be open to evolving ways of working in partnership in RJ.**
Support younger people when they integrate RJ principles and practices into how they lead and govern. Recognize and incorporate their ideas and collaborate to transform adult-dominated spaces.

• **Contribute to a multifaceted RJ movement by broadening the application and integration of restorative justice in other spaces.**
Build alliances and partnerships with people working to transform school systems and increase youth engagement (i.e., programs for leadership, student achievement, and college and career readiness). Integrate the principles of RJ into curriculum, incorporating ethnic studies, antiracist training, or critical pedagogy in schools and organizations.

- **Deepen the understanding that RJ is a practice and a way of being, both in and out of Circle.**
  Make time to have courageous conversations in Circle about healing, equity, unlearning history, and the implications of the First Harm, the genocide of Indigenous peoples, and the Second Harm of chattel slavery. Carry Circle practice into other areas of your lives, with family members, loved ones, and community members. Join affinity groups to discuss how your racial identity affords you privileges or disadvantages, and discuss how to make changes within yourself to push for equity in your life.

- **Advocate for funding and resources for youth engagement in RJ in schools to be sustainable.**
  Build infrastructure to support meaningful youth engagement and a pipeline of RJ leadership that becomes embedded in school and district cultures. Advocate that youth and elders are paid for their time and labor. Involve both youth and adult RJ practitioners in building relationships with funders and transforming funding streams.

- **Create time and space for continuous healing, celebration, and dreaming.**
  Ground RJ in the holistic well-being of self, community, and the planet. Create healing-centered spaces that incorporate food, the arts, games, music, movement, and the outdoors. Reflect and dream with others about how intergenerational partnerships in RJ can grow. Lean into joy and laughter, and embrace play.

105

- **Recognize that this is *life work* and requires praxis.**

  Liberation work is ongoing work, and the Spiral is one way that we, as the RJ community, can continuously engage in praxis. We call on youth and adults to dream together of what just and equitable schools can look like as we collectively move into action.

The Dream of Liberation

I remember my first Restorative Justice End of Year Ceremony, talking pieces were on the table and the word "Dream" stood out. I think about being able to chase dreams. There is a song lyric, "I dream chase like an athlete." Athletes work hard and go through challenges. Like a dream, you never have a straight path to reach something. Thinking about dreams makes me think about the bigger picture. . . . I always carry that talking piece in my backpack, in case it's needed. It was always there for me—reminding us to dream.

—*Samantha Pal, Oakland RJ leader*

In order for restorative justice in education to shift the dominant paradigm of power *over* to power *with*, the movement needs to listen, connect past and present, heal harms, value one another's contributions, and most importantly, like Samantha, dream. To "dream chase like an athlete"' is ongoing muscle building work. Athletes visualize, train, and practice their goals before they ever reach them. They push through challenges while learning to listen to their bodies.

106

Sam is a dancer; dancers are athletes, and like Circle keepers, they build muscles to listen, hold, and tell stories. Through reclaiming dances and languages that were robbed through colonization, many communities are building the muscle to dream. As a result of the Cambodian genocide by the Khmer Rouge, Sam's elders explained that their traditions were "stripped away" and they had to "hide who they were to survive." Through Circle and classical Khmer Robam (dance), Samantha is reclaiming her culture and identity; she transforms spaces with every movement of her fingertips. Sam reflects, "I didn't always understand the lyrics. But when I was dancing it all made sense. I started to find beauty. I now see how dance is storytelling."

To sustain individual and communal well-being in the movement for equitable schools, we urge RJ practitioners to envision a simultaneous dance of justice and joy. Youth and adults in intergenerational partnerships have the honor and responsibility to hold the past, present, and future, and to find moments to dream. Supaman, a hip-hop artist from the Crow Nation in Montana, reminds us that to dance leads us to be healed, affirmed, and finally, liberated:

Dance like everybody is watching. Dance like your children are watching, your ancestors, your family. Dance for those who are hurting, those who can't dance, those who lost loved ones and those who suffer injustices throughout the world. Let every step be a prayer for humanity![2]

Acknowledgments

We give gratitude to all who came before us in this movement, all who continue to teach and guide us, and all who come after us. We give special acknowledgement to Thomas Nikundiwe and Elizabeth "Betita" Martinez por su ejemplo que la lucha sigue y que juntos llegamos. You both modeled true intergenerational organizing that has influenced a generation to keep working for liberation.

We are grateful to our editor Barb Toews for her support and guidance, and Rha Bowden, Agustin "Base" Barajas-Amaral, and Stepani Slater for sharing their artistic talents.

Anita: Thank you to my ancestors in nameless villages in what is now Pakistan. Thank you, Varinder and Darshan, for giving me life and sustaining my physical, mental, and emotional being in the face of my own journey from self-hatred to self-love. Thank you to my comrades in Restorative Empowerment for Youth: Udoro Ekpin-Gatewood, Xavier Chavez, Leslie Lux, Angel Lagunas, Beatriz Macareno-Rodriguez, Esmeralda Rocha, Axcel Baltazar, Jermaine Williams, Kasandra Aviles, and Yancey Elguezabal—and all the young people I have had the honor to work with at Yes Prep Northbrook High and the Academy of Choice. Thank you to Thomas Nikundiwe for teaching me about liberation so many years ago. The world misses you. Thank you to Dev for being a model Mama for my daughters. Thank you, Suhani and Naya, for being my guides in living out restorative justice, and my husband Seth for, well, putting up with me and showing me what unconditional love and ongoing vulnerability look like.

Evelín: Deep gratitude to my ancestors, family, and friends for your endless love and support. I honor my abuelita, Ceferina Feliciano, and my mother, Juana, por tu inspiración, ejemplo y sabiduría. To my father, Juan Aquino, a living angel, I am forever grateful for our bond and your unconditional guidance to live a life of peace, love, creativity, and purpose. To my beloved children, Lani and Cielo, who light my way. To my husband, Lou, for your support. To Celi and my siblings for your encouragement. To Gramma and Grampa. To my nephew Malik. To my mentors: Elizabeth, Rose, Roberta, and Jacqui. To my community of fierce educators that walk their talk. To Bro/Sis, James, Safire, Clarke, JFHTHLC, EFC, Sayo, Beth, EBB. To all the young people I've ever worked with, you deeply inspire me. Thank you, Petua and Destiny. Gracias, Luke and Ro. Pa'lante—es mi honor caminar contigo! Seguimos todos firme—pa'lante siempre!

Heather: Gratitude to my family by blood and by love and to the lands and communities who continue to raise me. To my ancestors, including my comadre Isela and brother Sean. To my parents for sharing stories and unconditional love. To the thought partners, walkers, cooks, and editors who supported this journey: Anna, Adam, Bettina, Chen, Kellea, Sabrina, Steven, Taji, Xavi, Mike, and Mary. To Aeeshah Clottey for your guiding words, "If you can open a door, hold it open. Your role may not be to go through." To Mrs. Kashiwagi, who built authentic community with 1st graders. Deep gratitude to Itzamar Carmona, Denise Curtis, Arnoldo García, and Aurora Lopez for your wisdom and partnership in and out of Circle. Thank you to the RJ communities of Oakland, the OUSD intergenerational RJ crew, and all the young people I have had the honor to learn with and those who contributed to the creation of this book.

Bios

Evelín Aquino is a longtime organizer/educator/ trainer/dancer with over 35 years' experience of being in Circle with elders, peers, youth leaders, and community. Committed to education toward liberation, her work is grounded in love and relationships, while providing creative spaces for youth and adults to think critically, as they build together and take action as leaders in manifesting just and equitable schools. She holds the position of assistant director at Pa'lante RJ at Holyoke High School. She is a board member of the Encampment for Citizenship. Evelín is a Boricua/ Dominicana graduate of UMASS Amherst. She is deeply inspired and guided by the youth of today (especially her beloved children), her husband, family, and her ancestors and elders (especially her father).

Heather Bligh Manchester is an educator, trainer, and connector with over 30 years of experience facilitating leadership and community engagement programs and infusing theater, games, and movement into restorative justice in rural and urban settings, including the Oakland School District. She partners with youth and adults to create spaces for meaningful engagement to build equitable and resilient communities locally and internationally. Heather coaches organizations to work in partnership with young people as trainers, researchers, and policymakers. She has a Masters in Peace and Conflict Studies, with a focus on Youth Participation in Peacebuilding, from the University of Ulster. Rooted in family, nourished by travel, she thanks the stories that guide her.

Anita Wadhwa is a native Houstonian and daughter of Punjabi immigrants. She is a classroom teacher, trainer, and restorative justice coordinator. She is author of *Restorative Justice in Urban Schools: Disrupting the School to Prison Pipeline* and a contributor to the recently released anthology *Colorizing Restorative Justice*. She hires and consults with former students to train in restorative practices. She has developed a youth-led restorative justice model based on her research which has garnered national attention. She owes everything to her parents, husband, and two lovely girls.

Itzamar Carmona Felipe is an Oakland-raised Oakland Unified School District (OUSD) alum, born in Guerrero, Mexico. Throughout high school and college they worked in grassroots organizing focused on immigrant, housing, and worker rights and educational equity, specifically advocating for financial aid for undocumented undergrad students. They graduated from UC Santa Cruz with a bachelor's in sociology combined with Latin America and Latino studies and a minor in education. After graduating, they worked in OUSD as a restorative justice fellow supporting student engagement. They currently work on educational equity and youth organizing at a local nonprofit.

Recommended Readings

Fletcher, Adam F. C. *Student Voice Revolution: The Meaningful Student Involvement Handbook*. Olympia, WA: CommonAction Publishing, 2017.

Ginwright, Shawn, and Julio Cammarota. "New Terrain in Youth Development: The Promise of Social Justice Approach." *Social Justice*, 29(4), 2002.

Lewis, Ted, and Carl Stauffer. *Listening to the Movement: Essays on New Growth and New Challenges in Restorative Justice*. Eugene, OR: Cascade Books, 2021.

Love, Bettina L. *We Want to Do More Than Survive: Abolitionist Teaching and the Pursuit of Educational Freedom* United States: Beacon Press, 2019.

Manchester, Heather Bligh. "Youth Participation in Peacebuilding: Moving from Subjects to Partners." Master of Arts in Peace & Conflict Studies, University of Ulster, Magee Campus, 2010.

Pointer, Lindsey, Haley Farrar, and Kathleen McGoey. *The Little Book of Restorative Teaching Tools: Games, Activities, and Simulations for Integrating Restorative Justice Practices*. Intercourse, PA: Good Books, 2020.

Saad, Layla. *Me and White Supremacy: How to Recognise Your Privilege, Combat Racism and Change the World.* King of Prussia, PA: Quercus, 2020.

Shalaby, Carla. *Troublemakers: Lessons in Freedom From Young Children at School.* New York: The New Press, 2017.

Valandra, Edward (ed.), *Colorizing Restorative Justice: Voicing Our Realities.* St. Paul, MN: Living Justice Press, 2020.

Wadhwa, Anita. *Restorative Justice in Urban Schools: Disrupting the School-to-Prison Pipeline.* New York: Routledge, 2015.

Recommended Resources

- https://abolitionistteachingnetwork.org
- https://www.edliberation.org
- https://www.learningforjustice.org
- https://rethinkingschools.org
- https://www.zinnedproject.org
- https://courageousconversation.com
- https://www.raceforward.org
- http://yparhub.berkeley.edu

Endnotes

Introduction

1. Freire, Paulo. *Pedagogy of the Oppressed*. New York: Continuum, 2000.
2. Evans, K., Vaandering, D. (2016). *The Little Book of Restorative Justice in Education: Fostering Responsibility, Healing, and Hope in Schools*. New York: Good Books.

Chapter 1: The Field of Youth Engagement

1. Ginwright, Shawn, and Taj James. "From Assets to Agents of Change: Social Justice, Organizing, and Youth Development." *New Directions for Youth Development*, 2002. https://doi.org/10.1002/yd.25.
2. "YOUTH Participation 2013-11-12 - Un." Accessed June 30, 2021. https://www.un.org/esa/socdev/documents/youth/fact-sheets/youth-participation.pdf.
3. Checkoway, B., and L. Gutiérrez. "Youth Participation and Community Change." *Journal of Community Practice*, 2006.
4 Zeldin, Shepherd, Brian Christens, and Jane Powers. "The Psychology and Practice of Youth-Adult Partnership: Bridging Generations for Youth Development and Community Change." *American Journal of Community Psychology*, 2012. https://doi.org/https://doi.org/10.1007/s10464-012-9558-y.

5. Funders' collaborative on youth organizing. (2017). *Transforming Young People and Communities: New Findings on the Impacts of Youth Organizing.* https: //fcyo.org/resources/transforming-young-people -and-communities-new-findings-on-the-impacts-of -youth-organizing

6. Smith, Annie, Carly Hoogeveen, and Sarah Cotman. Rep. *A Seat at the Table: A Review of Youth Engagement in Vancouver,* 2009. http://mcs.bc.ca /pdf/A_Seat_at_the_Table2.pdf.

7. Fletcher, Adam. *The Guide to Student Voice: for Students, Teachers, Administrators, Advocates, and Others.* Olympia, WA.: CommonAction Consulting, 2013.

Chapter 2: Core Values: Intergenerational Partnerships and Liberatory Education

1. "Claudette Colvin: Twice Toward Justice." Zinn Education Project, March 2, 2021. https://www .zinnedproject.org/materials/claudette-colvin -twice-toward-justice/.

2. Dougherty, Ilona, ed. Rep. *The Youth-Friendly Guide to Intergenerational Decision-Making Partnerships,* 2004. https://www.ndi.org/sites/default/files/2061 _citpart_youth_010104_5.pdf.

3. Evans, Katherine, and Dorothy Vaandering. *The Little Book of Restorative Justice in Education: Fostering Responsibility, Healing, and Hope in Schools.* New York: Good Books, 2016.

4. Adapted from *Youth Adult Partnership Tips for Schools* created by OUSD intergenerational Restorative Justice Team, and All City Council Student Union. *Youth Adult Partnership Tips for Schools.* Oakland, CA: Oakland Unified School District—Restorative Justice, 2019.

5. The original iteration of this graphic is by Angus Maguire. There are dozens of reinterpretations of this diagram, and we believe this one comes closest to explaining the concept of liberation.
6. Freire, Paulo. *Pedagogy of the Oppressed*. New York: Continuum, 1993.

Chapter 3: Developing a Liberatory Consciousness

1. Leonen, Michael F., and Michael F. Leonen. "Etiquette for Activists." *YES!* Magazine, May 21, 2004. https://www.yesmagazine.org/issue/hope -conspiracy/2004/05/21/etiquette-for-activists.
2. Love, Barbara. "Developing a Liberatory Consciousness." Essay. In *Readings for Diversity and Social Justice*, edited by Maurianne Adams, Warren Blumenfeld, Carmelita Castañeda, Heather Hackman, Madeline Peters, and Ximena Zúñiga, 533–40. New York: Routledge, 2010.

Chapter 4: Laying the Foundation for Work with Youth: Anti-Adultism

1. Flasher, Jack. "Adultism." *Adolescence* 13, no. 51 (1978): 517–23.
2. Fletcher, Adam F.C. "What Everyday Adultism Looks Like." February 24, 2010. https://adamfletcher.net /2010/02/24/what-everyday-adultism-looks-like/.
3. Peeples, Tanesha. "School Discipline Is the Modern Day Chattel Slavery and Damn Near Everybody Is in on It." *Education Post*, March 6, 2021. https: //educationpost.org/school-discipline-is-the-modern -day-chattel-slavery-and-damn-near-everybody-is -in-on-it/.

4. Lansdown, Gerison (2005). The Evolving Capacities of the Child, *Innocenti Insights* no. 11.

Chapter 6: "Education, Liberation!": Apprenticing Youth as Restorative Justice Teachers

1. Janet was the first woman to participate in a Victim Offender Dialogue in Massachusetts after the murder of her son.

Chapter 7: ¡Sigue Pa'lante!: Collective Liberation in Holyoke

1. Zammataro. "Assata Shakur, Always Welcome." *The Advocate*, March 9, 2021. https://gcadvocate. com/2017/06/21/assata-shakur-always-welcome/.
2. "About." Palante. Accessed July 1, 2021. https: //palanteholyoke.org/about.
3. Springfield, MA—Our Plural History. Accessed June 30, 2021. http://ourpluralhistory.stcc.edu/industrial /irish.html.
4. Holyoke, MA—Holyoke Public Schools, July 20, 2021. https://www.hps.holyoke.ma.us/.
5. "About." Palante. Accessed June 30, 2021. https: //palanteholyoke.org/about.
6. "About." Palante. Accessed June 30, 2021. https: //palanteholyoke.org/about.
7. "El Corazón / The Heart of Holyoke." Patronicity. Accessed June 30, 2021. https://www.patronicity .com/project/el_corazn__the_heart_of_holyoke.

Chapter 8: Nothing about Us without Us: Youth, Justice, and Unity in Oakland

1. The following Oakland RJ Practitioners contributed through interviews, as thought partners and

editors to chapter 10 and 11: Nidia Baez, Meesh Cabal, Martha Calmo, Griffen Castillo, Sandy Chales, Tatiana Chaterji, Denise Curtis, Arnoldo García, Ta Biti Gibson, Natalie Gallegos Chavez, Fatima Gutierrez Ramirez, Brian Gil-Ríos, Juan Guillermo Pablo Matías, LeAna Hudson, Chen Kong-Wick, Linh Le, Aurora López, Ana Méndez, Vida Mendoza, Yota Omo-Sowho, Drew Owens, Samantha Pal, Jonathan Piper, Dani Primous, Maida Quintero Medrano, Siurave Quintanilla Vasquez, and Teresa Sot.

2. "Student, Family & Community Engagement Office: Student Engagement. Accessed June 30, 2021. https://www.ousd.org/Page/15546.

3. Omo-Sowho, Yota. 2019. "All City Council Student Director Report (Item K.19–0122)". Speech, OUSD Board of Education Meeting 2-13-19, 2019. http://ousd.legistar.com/gateway.aspx?M=F&ID=90660.pdf

4. "Local Control and Accountability Plan (LCAP)." Local Control and Accountability Plan (LCAP)—Resources (CA Dept of Education), 2021. https://www.cde.ca.gov/re/lc/.

5. Nothing About us without us! Youth Justice and Unity was the youth-created conference theme by Middle School ACC giving reference to a core OUSD RJ value, based on the slogan popularized by South African disability rights and youth activists, with historical roots in Eastern Europe.

6. OUSD. *OUSD Ethnic Studies Framework 2020–21*. OUSD, 2020. https://docs.google.com/document/d/1LhirYYX2gbnsdFfJ3G6LpE6lhUreaaUAeWFQeRNmemM/edit?ts=60c#.

7. Lopez, Aurora, and Kendra Fehrer. "Voices for Equity: Youth Leadership in Oakland Community Schools." In *Community Schools: People and Places Transforming Education and Communities*, edited by JoAnne Ferrara and Reuben Jacobson. Lanham, MD: Rowman & Littlefield, 2019.

8. Adams, Eric, and Wesley Sims. 2010. "10–0115 Presentation of Student Directors' Report January 27, 2010". Speech, Board of Education Meeting. Oakland, CA. http://ousd.granicus.com/player/clip/108?view_id=4&redirect=true

9. Hinton-Hodge, Jumoke, and Omo-Sowho, Yota. 2019. "Budget Policy Resolution Item C-1" OUSD Board of Education Meeting Minutes—March 4, 2019 http://ousd.legistar.com/gateway.aspx?M=F&ID=91058.pdf

10. Omo-Sowho, Yota. 2019. "All City Council Student Director Report (Item K.19–0122)". Speech, OUSD Board of Education Meeting 2-13-19, 2019. http://ousd.legistar.com/gateway.aspx?M=F&ID=90660.pdf

11. Stout, James. "The History of the Raised Fist, a Global Symbol of Fighting Oppression." History. National Geographic, May 3, 2021. https://www.nationalgeographic.com/history/article/history-of-raised-fist-global-symbol-fighting-oppression.

12. Artwork Rha Bowden www.eyemanifestsupreme.com

13. Davis, Fania. *The Little Book of Race and Restorative Justice: Black Lives, Healing, and US Social Transformation*. New York: Good Books, 2019.

14. The All City Council campaign hashtag for budget priorities to fight for funding for Restorative Justice.

Chapter 9: Youth Engagement in Restorative Justice: A Shifting Model of Leadership

1. Kaba, Mariama, Naomi Murakawa, and Tamara K. Nopper. *We Do This 'Til We Free Us: Abolitionist Organizing and Transforming Justice.* Chicago: Haymarket Books, 2021.
2. Artists and Circlekeepers Agustín "Base" Barajas-Amaral (Conch, Quetzalcoatl & Sankofa and Sunflower) and Rha Bowden (Circle & Fist, Lotus and Redwood Grove) created images in chapter 9.
3. The Quetzalcoatl and Sankofa in Circle was created by Agustín "Base" Barajas-Amaral to recognize RJ student leaders in Oakland schools and express the roots of Brown-Black unity.

Chapter 11: Intergenerational Partnerships for Liberation: A Call to Action

1. Valandra, Edward Charles, and Robert Yazzie. *Colorizing Restorative Justice: Voicing Our Realities.* St. Paul, MN: Living Justice Press, 2020.
2. G, About Paul. "Let Us Dance!"—New Supaman Video—July 22, 2016. https://www.powwows.com /let-us-dance-new-supaman-video/.